YORK NOTES

General Editors: Professor A.N. Jeffares (*University of Stirling*) & Professor Suheil Bushrui (*American University of Beirut*)

Sylvia Plath

SELECTED WORKS

Notes by Hana Sambrook
MA PH D (EDINBURGH)

LONGMAN
YORK PRESS

YORK PRESS
Immeuble Esseily, Place Riad Solh, Beirut.

LONGMAN GROUP UK LIMITED
Longman House, Burnt Mill, Harlow,
Essex CM20 2JE, England
Associated companies, branches and representatives
throughout the world

First published in 1990
Second impression 1992

ISBN 0-582-06563-1

Typeset by Gem Graphics, Trenance, Mawgan Porth, Cornwall
Printed in Hong Kong
WC/02

Contents

Part 1

Introduction

The life of Sylvia Plath

Sylvia Plath was born on 27 October 1932 in Jamaica Plain, Boston, Massachusetts, the first child of Otto and Aurelia Plath. Her father was a Professor of Entomology at Boston University, and her mother was a former student of his. Both the Plaths came of German-speaking stock; Otto was born at Grabowa in the Polish Corridor, while Aurelia's parents came from Austria. They both had all the virtues of their Central European background – thrift, the capacity to work hard, a deep respect for education and for intellectual achievement. Sylvia, or 'Sivvy', as she was called at home, was everything such parents could have wished for. An attractive, sturdy child, highly intelligent and articulate, she seemed to sense instinctively that intellectual achievement was the surest way to gain her parents' approval. From a tiny child she was an 'achiever': ambitious, always striving to do well, to be the best, to gain praise and popularity.

After the birth of her second child, Warren, Mrs Plath had less time for her first-born, who came to be cared for more and more by her maternal grandparents. In their house the little girl found herself cherished and encouraged as much as she had been at home. When in due course she started school, her ability and self-confidence stood her in good stead, and she found adjustment easy.

There were sad changes ahead, though. Otto Plath's health deteriorated alarmingly, and he became convinced that he had cancer. Surprisingly for a man of his intelligence and scientific background he refused to consult a doctor. Only when an injury to his toe resulted in gangrene was a doctor called in. He diagnosed diabetes mellitus which if spotted earlier could have been treated quite easily. As it was, the gangrene was too advanced, a drastic amputation had to be carried out, and Otto Plath did not survive the resultant complications. He died in November 1940. When told of his death, Sylvia declared passionately that she would never speak to God again, but after this one outburst she insisted on going to school and behaving as if nothing had happened.

Otto Plath's death left the family in desperate financial straits, and Mrs Plath had to work full-time as a teacher to support herself and her children who thus found themselves doubly bereaved – they had lost their father, and their mother could no longer devote herself to them in daytime. To fill her place, Mrs Plath's parents came to live with the family. In 1942 Mrs Plath was offered a post at Boston University, and the family moved to Wellesley, an attractive upper-class community for which the Paths were ill-suited financially.

Life was beset by anxieties; Mrs Plath suffered from gastric ulcers and had two lengthy spells in hospital. Sylvia's academic record at high school, however, must have been a constant source of satisfaction. She did extremely well in all subjects (except sewing!), was good at sports and extracurricular activities, and had a number of poems published, first in the school magazine and later in national magazines and newspapers.

In her last year at high school Sylvia decided to apply for admission to Smith College, a prestigious women's college at Northampton, Massachusetts. She was awarded two scholarships for her first year, one of them funded by Mrs Olive Higgins Prouty, a successful novelist, who became Sylvia's lifelong friend and benefactress. As these scholarships were awarded yearly only, Sylvia was never entirely free of financial anxiety while at Smith.

Nevertheless she was blissfully happy in her first year at college (1950–1). There was the sense of achievement, of being 'a Smith woman'; there was also the pleasure of working under the constant intellectual stimulus of her teachers, and the delight of making friends with other students at Smith. Given the American system of 'dating', which rates a girl's popularity by the number of men who have asked her on a date, there was also some uneasiness. Sylvia had never been outstandingly popular with boys at high school, perhaps because she intimidated by her intelligence, and was never able to hide that other self, the Sylvia of her poems, beneath the image she presented to the world of the leggy, sun-tanned blonde who smiles so broadly in all her photographs. She needed a man who would impress her Smith friends, girls from a secure financial background, with an abundant supply of dates from the same upper-class society. The answer to Sylvia's problems was Dick Norton, a childhood friend from Wellesley, who invited her to Yale for a weekend. The relationship pleased her and calmed her fears of being left out, but it seems doubtful whether her emotions were deeply involved.

Her sophomore (second) year at Smith (1951–2) went equally well, and she was successful in placing her short stories and poems; in addition she won a fiction prize from *Mademoiselle*, a magazine for young women with a clear 'upmarket' image.

Her junior (third) year at Smith (1952–3) started badly. For financial reasons she had to move to one of the 'scholarship houses' where students worked (cleaning, preparing food) in return for part of their boarding costs. Her work was not going well, she was uncertain about what she wanted from life, unsure about her relationship with Dick Norton. Her spirits rose, however, when in the spring term she learned that she had won a guest editorship on *Mademoiselle*, to live in New York for four weeks at the magazine's expense while working on its editorial staff. Only twenty women students were chosen from colleges all over the country, and the boost to Sylvia's morale was considerable.

After four hectic weeks in New York she went home for the summer, only to discover that she had not been accepted for a summer fiction course at Harvard on which she had set her heart. Her depression grew worse, aggravated by severe insomnia. She felt totally inadequate to face the strain of the coming final year at college, and began to think of suicide. She cut her legs 'to see if [she] had the guts', and was sent for psychiatric treatment which included painful electric shock therapy.

After one such treatment, in her family's absence, she took a bottle of her mother's sleeping-pills and crawled into the floorspace under the house where she consumed all the pills. On the third day after her disappearance her brother discovered her in her hiding place, half-conscious. She was taken to hospital where she recovered physically, but her mental state continued to cause anxiety and she was transferred first to a psychiatric hospital, and then, at Mrs Prouty's expense, to a private hospital where she gradually recovered.

She returned to Smith for the spring term. She was now something of a celebrity at college, embarked on a series of love affairs, and grew more and more successful as a writer, having had a number of short stories and poems published. Academic success was hers as well. She had been awarded a major scholarship by Smith to enable her to complete her course, and she graduated *summa cum laude* and won a Fulbright scholarship to Newnham College, Cambridge.

She sailed for England in September 1955, and by October was settled and happy at Cambridge. Her letters home may read like the gushings of an American tourist, but, in fact, she was now beginning to find her true poetical voice.

In February 1956 she met and fell in love with the man she was to marry, the poet Ted Hughes, her 'violent Adam'. Hughes, a Yorkshireman, was a Cambridge graduate in anthropology, now making his name as the foremost poet of his generation while working as reader for the J. Arthur Rank film company and doing occasional work for the BBC.

Her relationship with Hughes absorbed Sylvia totally, even while she was travelling in Europe with old American boyfriends. In a letter to her brother she spoke of her yearning 'to find [her] voice in writing', in order to express her joy of 'living like mad'. She was in love, was enjoying her work, and finding her way into the Cambridge literary circle, having joined the staff of *Varsity* magazine.

Her mother came over to visit her in June 1956 and three days after her arrival found herself attending her daughter's secret wedding in London. Sylvia concealed her marriage for some time, because she was afraid that as a married woman she might lose her Fulbright scholarship. The plan was that she would continue to live in college while her husband pursued his writing career in London. By October 1956, however, the strain of living separately became intolerable for them both. In the end the college authorities proved sympathetic, and Sylvia was allowed to complete her year while living with her husband in a small flat not far from Newnham.

She took up her role as a housewife with enthusiasm while still working for her examinations. Naturally there were pressures: Sylvia the achiever and perfectionist wanted to excel in her domestic duties as well as in her academic career. She suffered some anxiety about the future as well, but her old college, Smith, came to the rescue, offering her a teaching post for a year. At the same time her husband won the book prize of the New York Poetry Society for his collection of verse, *The Hawk in the Rain*, even before the book was published.

In early June 1957 Sylvia took her final examinations at Cambridge and was awarded a second-class degree, a disappointment to her. A few weeks later she and Ted sailed to America.

Her job at Smith proved far more demanding than she had anticipated. She found it difficult to communicate her own enthusiasm for literature to her students, and to control the classroom. The strain of teaching as well as keeping house was too great, and she found that she had no time for her own writing. Ted, meanwhile, was writing steadily and getting his work published, and his wife began to grudge him his leisure to write and his success.

Against her mother's wishes Sylvia decided to resign from her post at the end of the academic year. She and Ted would take a small apartment in Boston for a year and concentrate on their writing in the hope of winning study grants on the strength of it.

To begin with this plan seemed destined to fail, as far as Sylvia was concerned. She was suffering from writer's block (that is, she was unable to write), depressed to the point of seeking psychiatric help, worried about finances and taking secretarial jobs to ease this anxiety. Gradually, however, matters improved. She joined a poetry workshop at Boston University, taught by the poet Robert Lowell, and made friends with other students at the workshop, especially with the poet Anne Sexton. Soon Sylvia found herself writing short stories and poems again, and getting them published.

She and Ted decided to return to England, but first, in summer 1959, they spent two months at a writers' colony in Yaddo, Saratoga Springs, in New York State. Free of domestic duties, she felt at ease and had no problems with her writing: her collection *The Colossus and Other Poems* was started at Yaddo. Moreover, she was pregnant and was feeling fit and well.

The Hugheses started for England in December 1959, and early in 1960 they moved into a small flat in Chalcot Square, near Primrose Hill in north London. This was a good year for Sylvia: in February 1960 the publishing firm of William Heinemann agreed to publish *The Colossus*, in March Ted's *Lupercal* came out, and his book for children, *Meet My Folks*, followed. Their financial situation improved, especially when Ted's *The Hawk in the Rain* won the Somerset Maugham Award, just in time for their baby's arrival.

Frieda Rebecca was born on 1 April 1960. Though the Hugheses still managed to attend literary parties together, the burden of caring for the baby fell on Sylvia, and she began to feel increasingly tired and depressed, though she still managed to find a little time for her own writing.

The following year, 1961, brought more stress. In February she suffered a miscarriage, and later the same month she had to have an appendectomy. These setbacks were compensated for by a favourable contract for Sylvia with the prestigious *New Yorker* magazine, and further successes for Ted, bringing encouragement and financial help, and enabling Sylvia to start on her novel *The Bell Jar*.

Both she and her husband now felt that London with its distractions of literary society was not the place for them if they wished to concentrate on their writing. Also, Sylvia was pregnant again, and the London flat was clearly going to be too small for a growing family. They found a house they liked in North Devon, and moved there at the end of August 1961. Their new home was a charming old house, but it lacked all the modern conveniences to which Sylvia had been accustomed in America. Yet, in spite of the demands of housekeeping and her pregnancy, she still found time to write verse and finish her novel.

Her second child, Nicholas Farrar, was born on 17 January 1962, and, astonishingly, while running a large, inconvenient house and looking after two young children, Sylvia found the time to write a radio play, *Three Women* (published in *Winter Trees*), inspired by her experiences of childbirth and miscarriage. She wrote poetry too, filled with unease and anger; her husband was frequently absent from home, and Sylvia was jealous and resentful (the incident of her burning her husband's papers in a fit of jealous rage is often quoted). Her writing grew more and more important to her – as a possible source of income and material independence, and, especially, as a means of establishing her own unique personality, independent of Ted. She seemed to be preparing herself for what was to follow.

By September 1962 it was clear that she and her husband had drifted apart, and Sylvia decided on a legal separation (later she was to change her mind and ask for a divorce). Her husband finally moved out in September 1962, and Sylvia turned to her writing. Out of her pain and anger came the poems she assembled in November for publication as *Ariel* (to be published posthumously). She decided to leave the Devon house and return to London.

She found a flat, again in the Primrose Hill area of London, in Fitzroy Road, in a house where the Irish poet W. B. Yeats had lived, and in early December she and the children moved to London.

The New Year began badly: both she and the children fell ill with flu and colds, during one of the worst winters London had ever known. The publication of *The Bell Jar* brought some comfort, but did not lift the deep depression from which Sylvia was suffering after her illness. Her doctor tried to persuade her to accept hospital treatment, but with her painful memories of electric shock treatments at the psychiatric hospital she refused.

On 11 February 1963 Sylvia Plath rose early, put the children's breakfast milk beside their cots, and went into the kitchen. With her customary efficiency she sealed the doors with tape and placed towels under them so that no gas could escape into the children's room. She then took an overdose of sleeping-pills, turned on the gas on the kitchen stove, and lay down with her head inside the oven, having left a note in which she asked that her own doctor be called. She was found dead by a nurse sent by her doctor. An inquest was held and the verdict was that she 'did kill herself'.

Her status as a writer had grown steadily in her lifetime, but the manner of her death brought an upsurge of interest, not altogether literary, in her work. Seen then as a symbol of romantic self-destruction, she was later hailed by the feminist movement in the late sixties and seventies as a victim of a male-oriented society. Her life and death roused passionate emotions of both adulation and disapproval, but her poetry stands apart. It rose out of her anger and misery, yet it asks to be judged on its own very considerable merits.

A note on the text

Ariel was first published posthumously in London by Faber in 1965. The paperback edition, used in the preparation of these Notes, appeared in 1968.

Other poems discussed in these Notes are from *The Colossus and*

Other Poems (William Heinemann, London, 1960; Faber, London, 1967; paperback by Faber, 1972), *Crossing the Water* (Faber, London, 1971; paperback 1975) and *Winter Trees* (Faber, London, 1971; paperback 1975). For these poems, too, the paperback editions of the above collections have been used. All of the poems studied are available in *Collected Poems*, edited by Ted Hughes (Faber, London, 1981).

The Bell Jar was first published under a pseudonym, Victoria Lucas, in 1963 by William Heinemann, and reissued in paperback under Plath's own name by Faber in 1966. Again these Notes are based on the paperback edition.

Part 2

Summaries
of SELECTED WORKS

Note: As well as the entire *Ariel* volume and Sylvia Plath's only novel, *The Bell Jar*, these Notes also discuss a number of poems from her other collections. These have been chosen for their significance for any assessment of Plath's work, but inevitably they also reflect the present writer's personal preferences. They are all contained in *Collected Poems*, edited by Ted Hughes (Faber, London, 1981).

Ariel

Morning Song

Written after her daughter's birth, the poem records the actual moment of the child's birth. The mother feels her own separateness and insignificance beside the baby. She wakes in the night, listening to the baby's breathing, and goes to her when she cries. Morning comes and the baby begins to cry in earnest.

NOTES AND GLOSSARY:

In a drafty museum: the naked baby resembles a small statue in a museum. Sylvia Plath often uses this image (see 'Last Words' in *Crossing the Water*, 'All the Dead Dears' in *The Colossus*)

among the flat pink roses: in a room papered with a pattern of roses

A far sea moves in my ear: in the silence of the night she hears the blood singing in her ears

Your mouth opens clean as a cat's: the words capture the sharp, neat shape of a cat's mouth

Whitens and swallows its dull stars: it is daybreak and the stars disappear one by one

The Couriers

This poem was written after the breakdown of her marriage, and reflects her bitter distrust of the future as well as a defiant expression of her hope of happiness to come. The couriers seem to be the carriers of secret signs foretelling the future. The poet examines and rejects them in turn: a snail's trail, an alien sign; sourness; a wedding ring which promises faithfulness and betrays; a frosted leaf, symbol of isolation; the broken mirror of the sea foretelling ill luck; and lastly love, her chosen fate.

NOTES AND GLOSSARY:

Acetic acid: constituent from which the sourness of vinegar is derived

nine black Alps: there is an echo of this curious image in *The Bell Jar*, Chapter 7, 'a little white Alp at the back of my eye'

The sea shattering its grey one: the moving surface of the sea looks like a broken mirror (which, we should remember, brings bad luck)

Sheep in Fog

A depressing foggy day, full of threat. The depression affects the poet; she feels herself disapproved of, threatened.

NOTES AND GLOSSARY:

The hills step off into whiteness: the thick white fog cuts off the line of the hills abruptly

A flower left out: a flower blackened by frost

a heaven/Starless and fatherless, a dark water: as so often in Plath's poetry, water is a symbol of death here, death with no afterlife

---

The Applicant

Written in the last autumn of her life, the poem is full of vicious rage against men and the conventional idea of a good wife. The applicant in search of a wife is interviewed to decide if he is sufficiently weak and empty-headed to need a wife who would make up all his deficiencies. According to Plath the poem was written to be read aloud, and it certainly gains by being spoken aloud and fast, like a salesman's patter, with a strong emphasis on the repetitions.

NOTES AND GLOSSARY:

To thumb shut your eyes: a dead person's eyes are closed by smoothing down the lids

new stock from the salt: new wives from the tears of the old ones; there may be an oblique reference here to Lot's wife, who was turned into a pillar of salt for her curiosity (Genesis 19:26)

I have the ticket for that: a rephrasing of 'just the ticket', something just right

she'll be silver . . . gold: the silver and golden anniversaries of the wedding

---

Lady Lazarus

A harshly mocking poem boasting of the poet's ability to survive accidents and suicide attempts. It combines the biblical story of Lazarus with horrifying images of the Nazi concentration camps.

NOTES AND GLOSSARY:

Lazarus: we find the story of Lazarus whom Jesus raised from the dead in the Bible, John 11

A Nazi lampshade: one of the most appalling facts to emerge from the trials of Nazi war criminals was that a concentration camp commandant had lampshades made of human skin

My right foot/A paper weight: an elaboration of the lampshade horror

My face a featureless, fine/Jew linen: the corpse of Lazarus was 'bound head and foot with graveclothes: and his face was bound about with a napkin' (John 11:44), but the reference to 'Jew linen' returns to the terrible events of the twentieth century

The grave cave ate: notice the disorienting effect of the repetition of vowels

This is Number Three: if the poem is autobiographical, it is not clear what Number One had been (Number Two was obviously the suicide attempt in 1953, and Number Three a car accident in which Plath was involved in summer 1962)

The peanut-crunching crowd: the resurrected woman becomes a funfair freak exhibit

The first time it happened I was ten: there is no reference to any such event in the biographies of Sylvia Plath

They had to call and call: at the time of Plath's suicide attempt a search was made for her in the woods round Wellesley

Herr Doktor . . . Herr Enemy: the (German) psychiatrist

Ash, ash: it is impossible not to remember the gas ovens when reading this and the following stanza. Remember that human fat was turned into soap at Auschwitz and other death camps, and that the victims' rings and gold fillings were collected

Out of the ash: the myth of the Phoenix is recalled here; this fabulous bird burns itself to death and rises singing out of its ashes

And I eat men like air: because of the ambiguity of the word 'man' in the English language this line can be interpreted as either a feminist declaration or a hostile threat to all mankind

Tulips

Written in 1961 after Plath's miscarriage and appendectomy. A woman lying in her hospital bed looks at the red tulips sent by her husband. Their bright red colour does not fit into the white, peaceful emptiness of the hospital room. Like the photographs of her husband and children the flowers disturb her, trying to pull her back to her normal life, away from the peace of the hospital.

NOTES AND GLOSSARY:

my teaset, my bureaus of linen, my books: symbols of the different aspects of her life: her friends, her household tasks, her writing

a cut-paper shadow: this image of people as cut-out paper silhouettes appears also in 'Crossing the Water'

Cut

Dedicated to Susan, the young nurse who looked after Sylvia Plath's children after the break-up of her marriage. The poem is a quick succession of sensations and images, mostly of war and violence, written after the poet had cut her thumb when cooking.

NOTES AND GLOSSARY:

Little pilgrim: the Pilgrim Fathers, the original New England settlers, fought the Indians for the land

Your turkey wattle/Carpet: the blood. There is a play on words here: turkey the bird (eaten by Americans at Thanksgiving dinner, the fourth Thursday in November, in memory of the Pilgrim Fathers), and Turkey carpet, a soft thick carpet, often red

Redcoats: Redcoats was the nickname given to the British soldiers during the American War of Independence; here it also means red blood cells

Homunculus: tiny artificially produced man

Kamikaze man: Japanese airman making a suicidal attack on an enemy ship

Ku Klux Klan: American secret society founded at the end of the Civil War to terrorise black people. Its members wear hooded white robes

Babushka: headsquare worn by Russian peasant women

Trepanned veteran: soldier with a head wound which necessitated the removal of part of the skull

---

Elm

Dedicated to Ruth Fainlight, the American poet and wife of the English novelist Alan Sillitoe. In the poem the elm is female and speaks with a woman's voice. She knows about death, about madness. She knows too that love is only passing; the sound of her branches is the throb of passion. She has experienced flaming sunsets, destructive gales, the hard light of the moon. The tree lives in the poet's bad dreams, and in it lies hidden the desire for love. She does not wish to know more, for knowledge kills.

NOTES AND GLOSSARY:

tap root: the strong main root of a tree which goes vertically into the ground

being barren: the moon, traditionally of the female gender, is like a barren woman, it can give no life

flat, as after radical surgery: flat-chested like a woman after mastectomy, the removal of a cancerous breast

Nightly it flaps out: the image is that of an owl looking for its prey at night

So murderous in its strangle of branches: the creature, with its 'snaky acids', recalls the serpent in the Tree of Knowledge in the Bible (Genesis 3)

That kill, that kill, that kill: as elsewhere Plath uses repetition for a purpose, to stress the inevitability

---

The Night Dances

A poem about remembering ephemeral happy moments with a child.

NOTES AND GLOSSARY:

In mathematics: in cold matter-of-factness

I shall not entirely/Sit emptied of beauties: I shall not forget the happy times

the calla . . . the tiger: two kinds of lily, very different from each

other; the calla has stiff white folded flowers while the tiger lily is orange with black spots
the black amnesias of heaven: the coldness of the vast sky which remembers nothing, against the warmth of human memories

Poppies in October

The unseasonal appearance of poppies so late in the year seems a surprise gift.

NOTES AND GLOSSARY:
Igniting its carbon monoxides: the sky above the choked town traffic, full of petrol fumes
O my God, what am I: the poet is humbled by the splendour of this gift

Berck-Plage

Although the poem's title locates it in a small French seaside resort south of Boulogne, which Plath visited with her husband in 1961, its deepest inspiration was the death of Percy Key, a Devonshire friend. Sylvia Plath came down from London for his funeral in June 1962, at a time when her marriage was already breaking up.

Part I offers a nightmare vision of the seaside, made ugly and menacing by the poet's overwrought imagination.

Part II again consists of a series of ugly images: the priest's black boot is a coffin for his dead foot (we remember here Otto Plath's amputated leg); the sand dunes hide women in obscene bikinis; there are lovers coupling behind a bunker, watched by an excited onlooker.

Images of death and sickness predominate in Part III, inspired by the sanatoria at Berck-Plage. The poet has no sympathy to offer. A description of an operation on a dying old man is obviously based on the long-drawn-out illness and operation undergone by Percy Key, and the remaining sections of the poem tell of his funeral.

A horrifying description of a corpse in his coffin is the main subject of Part IV. Beautified by the mortician, he looks unreal. The linen of his deathbed has already been laundered, and the neighbours come to offer the usual trite words of comfort.

In Part V the widow sits in her house, thinking of practical matters while a curtain in the open window flickers like the dead man's tongue, pleading to be remembered.

In Part VI the funeral procession moves to the churchyard and the priest goes forward to receive it. The freshly dug earth of the grave is the colour of dried blood. The widow and her daughters stand by the side of the grave among the wreaths. The flowers seem to be intended for a wedding in which the dead man's soul is the bride, waiting to be received by the bridegroom, the newly dug red earth.

In Part VII the poet is one of the mourners riding to the churchyard behind the hearse. Watched by children, six bearers carry the coffin to the grave. There is no hope, death is final.

NOTES AND GLOSSARY:

A sandy damper: the sand acts as a damper on a piano, reducing the sound

the shrunk voices/Waving and crutchless: images of sickness, of abnormality, incongruous for a seaside crowd

the black and green lozenges: the pattern on the mackerel bodies

that crystallized these: these lozenges, from being the pattern on the fishes' backs, become the sweets of the same name

the hearse of a dead foot: understandably Plath is obsessed by the horror of amputation

Two lovers unstick themselves: there is a sexual revulsion in the image, as there is in the final image of this Part, of a seaweed resembling the genitals with pubic hair

This is the side of a man: the man on the operating table is like a piece of butcher's meat (Percy Key had an unsuccessful operation for lung cancer)

Where are the eye-stones . . .: both sight and speech are gone

like touched gardenias: gardenias turn brown if handled carelessly

propped his jaw with a book: supported the dropped jaw (due to the slackening of the muscles after death) until rigor mortis set in

The empty benches of memory look over stones: the dead are forgotten

jelly-glassfuls of daffodils: jam-jars filled with daffodils on the graves, a homely, accurate detail

Pollarded: with the tops cut off to encourage the growth of new branches

pocketbook: (*US*) handbag

A tarred fabric: the priest's black cassock

A crest of breasts, eyelids and lips: the bright curves of the wreaths on the coffin seem like the outline of a woman's body

the melt of shoe-blacking: the phrase evokes the formal, rarely worn black suits of the mourners

Six round black hats . . . mouth: the six bearers, the wooden coffin

and the open grave. The lines seem almost like a
child's riddle

plasma: liquid compound of blood

Ariel

The poet feels herself lifted out of darkness into light as she rides her
horse. She is transformed into an arrow, shedding old claims and
limitations, finding her own direction. The poem is justifiably
claimed by feminists as a declaration of personal freedom even from
those ties which are traditionally held sacrosanct.

NOTES AND GLOSSARY:

Ariel: in Hebrew the word means 'God's lion', but
mainly through the influence of William Shakespeare's (1564–1616) *Tempest* (1611) it has come
to mean a spirit of the air, genderless. It was also
the name of the horse Sylvia Plath rode in Devon

Stasis: period of inactivity

tor: Devonshire name for a rocky hill

The brown arc/Of the neck: her horse's neck

Godiva: the legendary wife of Leofric, who rode naked
through the streets of Coventry to make her
husband lift the excessive taxes he had imposed
on his tenants

Dead hands, dead stringencies: memories, emotional claims of the
past

The child's cry/Melts in the wall: she does not heed the claims of her
children

Death & Co.

A poem of terror, written in the last autumn of Plath's life. To her,
death takes two forms. One, the traditional unsmiling figure, scarred,
eager for flesh like a bird of prey. He tells her that her time has not
yet come, makes fun of her, contrasts her appearance with the pretty
dead babies in the hospital mortuary. The other death smiles, keeps
his hair fashionably long, smokes, can be sexually aroused, wants to
be loved. The flowers painted by frost on glass, the glitter of the
dewdrop, all speak of death.

NOTES AND GLOSSARY:

like Blake's: William Blake (1757–1827), English poet and
engraver, illustrated his mystical works with his

own designs. His figures have characteristic
bulging eyes. Sylvia Plath was reading Blake in
autumn 1962 when she wrote this poem
The nude/Verdigris of the condor: the condor's bald neck is given the
greenish shade of discoloured copper, a peculiarly
repulsive image
the flutings of their Ionian/Death-gowns: the folds of the babies'
shrouds resemble the flutings of columns in the
Greek Ionian style
plausive: pleasing
Masturbating a glitter: creating a false sexual excitement
Somebody's done for: the use of contemporary slang for dramatic
effect is characteristic of Plath

Nick and the Candlestick

Presumably written in early 1962, after the birth of her son Nicholas.
Awake in the night, the poet is filled with terror, but the sight of the
sleeping baby steadies her.

NOTES AND GLOSSARY:
I am a miner: sitting by a lighted candle she sees herself as a
miner, carrying his candle to warn him of the
presence of gases by the changes in the flame
Black bat airs . . . raggy shawls,/Cold homicides: all images of gloom
and terror
Old cave of calcium/Icicles: the drops of melted wax on the candle are
like stalactites. The image, first introduced in the
second line of the poem, now widens to become a
whole cave, in which even the newts and the fish
are white
holy Joes: pious hypocrites
A piranha/Religion: the white fish in the white cave become the
symbols of a cruel religion. The piranhas are
ferocious South American fish capable of strip-
ping the flesh clean off the bones of their victims.
The blood drawn by the fish becomes the blood as
wine of Holy Communion
O embryo/Remembering: the baby still sleeps in the foetal position
hung our cave with roses: the rose-patterned wallpaper mentioned
also in 'Morning Song', which too contains
references to cosy Victoriana
You are the baby in the barn: perhaps a reference to Christ's
birth

Gulliver

This poem is inspired by the famous passage in Chapter 1 of Jonathan Swift's (1667–1745) satire *Gulliver's Travels* (1726). After a shipwreck the eponymous hero wakes up on an island, the kingdom of Lilliput, inhabited by tiny people. While asleep, he had been tied by innumerable silk threads to the ground so that he can see nothing but the sky. His plight is used as a symbol of a poet's striving after his vision, while obstructed by small-minded, envious people. The poem has also been interpreted as an image of her husband's capture by those unworthy of him.

NOTES AND GLOSSARY:

With no strings attached: this colloquial idiom, meaning 'no limitations, no conditions', is here taken up and used literally

The spider-men: the phrase expresses not just their minute size, but also the spitefulness of their small minds

they are inch-worms: the use of an insect image parallels a line in 'The Colossus' ('I crawl like an ant')

They would have you sleep in their cabinets: they want you dead, chopped up and displayed in museums

Crivelli: Carlo Crivelli (*c*.1435–93), Italian painter. Plath may have seen his *Annunciation* in the National Gallery in London

Getting There

An extended metaphor of a train transporting the wounded from the battlefield is used here to symbolise pain and regeneration. The images seem to be more of the First World War with its great set battles in the mud of the trenches than of the Second World War.

NOTES AND GLOSSARY:

Krupp: name of a famous family of German arms manufacturers important in both world wars

faucet: (*US*) water-tap

Pumped ahead by these pistons: the movement of the pistons merges with the pumping action of the heart, moving the blood round the body

mud on my feet,/Thick, red and slipping: the bloody mud of the trenches

It is Adam's side: an image of birth; see the biblical story of the creation of woman from Adam's rib (Genesis 2:21–3)

Mourned by religious figures, by garlanded children: a tomb in a church, surrounded by paintings and statues, suggests this image

The carriages rock, they are cradles: an image of regeneration

Lethe: in Greek mythology the river of forgetfulness from which souls drank to forget their previous existence before reincarnation

---

Medusa

Entitled in draft 'Mum: Medusa', the poem is a vicious attack on the poet's mother. Ironically, on the very day when Plath wrote this poem (16 October 1962), she also wrote two letters home frantically begging for help (though, significantly, she asked if her aunt or sister-in-law could come over to help her, not her mother).

NOTES AND GLOSSARY:

your unnerving head: in Greek mythology Medusa was one of the three Gorgons, women with snakes in their hair who could turn into stone anyone who looked at them. Perseus killed Medusa using a mirror so that he did not need to look at her as he cut off her head

Your stooges/Plying their wild cells: perhaps the ties of blood

rip tide: tidal stretch of disturbed water

Old barnacled umbilicus: the umbilical cord which links the baby in the womb with its mother and is cut at birth is equated here with the telephone cable laid on the sea-bottom to link Europe with America; it is no doubt encrusted with barnacles

dazzling and grateful,/Touching and sucking: the adjectives illustrate the different aspects of mother love, its shining emotion, its gratitude for a child's response, its eagerness for physical contact, and, lastly, its power to draw in the child

Fat and red, a placenta: mark the tone of loathing of the physical tie of childbirth

Blubbery Mary: a cruelly mocking description of the Virgin Mary weeping at the foot of the Cross

I shall take no bite of your body: I refuse your self-sacrifice

Bottle in which I live: her mother keeps her like a dead baby in a

preserving liquid. The image clearly fascinated
Plath: see 'Two Views of a Cadaver Room' in *The
Colossus*, and 'Stillborn' in *Crossing the Water*,
and indeed the central metaphor of *The Bell Jar*

Green as eunuchs, your wishes/Hiss at my sins: her mother's
disapproval of any sexual aberration enrages the
daughter

There is nothing between us: a flat denial of any links of love,
chillingly effective

The Moon and the Yew Tree

Describing the view from the Devonshire house at night, the poem
quickly becomes a bleak statement of nothingness, of despair. The
yew tree, which figures also in 'Little Fugue', seems linked in the
poet's mind with the figure of her dead father.

NOTES AND GLOSSARY:
the light of the mind, cold and planetary: as elsewhere in Plath's
poetry the moon is seen as emotionally cold,
barren (see 'Elm' and 'The Rival')
I simply cannot see where there is to get to: a denial of afterlife
the O-gape: the mouth opens in the shape of the letter O;
there is undoubtedly an intentional echo here of
the Greek *agape*, selfless love, the love feast
Her blue garments: blue is traditionally the Virgin Mary's colour
blackness and silence: death with no afterlife

A Birthday Present

Addressed perhaps to her husband, the poem seems to be a plea for
truth. The present stands veiled, watching her as she goes about her
housework. Let the telling of truth be her birthday present; he need
not fear that she will create a scene, she will accept it quietly. She
cannot bear the uncertainty and wants to be told at once. Even if such
a truth is death to her, it will pierce her cleanly.

NOTES AND GLOSSARY:
has it breasts, has it edges?: is it soft and kind, or hard and cruel?
it is just what I want: an ironical use of the cliché of present-receiving
the one for the annunciation: a clear echo, undoubtedly ironical, of
the Annunciation, the coming of the Archangel
Gabriel to the Virgin Mary to tell her that she has
been chosen to be the mother of the Messiah

My God, what a laugh: another example of Plath's effective use of slang, a harsh and jarring intrusion into the solemn scene
I am alive only by accident: probably a reference to the car accident Plath had in September 1962
come by the mail, finger by finger: an allusion to the newspaper stories of kidnap victims' fingers being cut off and sent to their families to show them that the death threat is real
And the universe slide from my side: and I would die

Letter in November

The poet walks in her orchard, squelching through the wet grass, happy but conscious of the wounds the past has dealt her.

NOTES AND GLOSSARY:
the wall of old corpses: the old churchyard by the Hugheses' house in Devon
a thick grey death-soup: the fog
the mouths of Thermopylae: Thermopylae is a mountain pass in Greece, the site of a famous battle in 480BC in which Leonidas with his Spartan army defended the pass against the Persians at the cost of all their lives

---

The Rival

It has been suggested that the woman attacked here so viciously is Sylvia Plath's mother, against whom Plath was always measuring herself. The mention of regular letters in the third stanza does seem to corroborate this interpretation. If there is a hint of sexual rivalry in the poem, perhaps the ambiguity lay in the relationship itself: the daughter competing with her mother for her father's attention.

NOTES AND GLOSSARY:
If the moon smiled: another example of Plath's image of the moon as cold, barren and destructive (see for instance 'Elm', 'The Moon and the Yew Tree')
Both of you are great light borrowers: the moon takes her reflected light from the sun
Her O-mouth: the O-gape of 'The Moon and the Yew Tree'
Arrive through the mailslot with loving regularity: a devastating description of her mother's regular letters

expansive as carbon monoxide: carbon monoxide (also mentioned in 'A Birthday Present') is a poisonous gas found in coal gas. Thoughts of it were present in Plath's mind, and we should remember that this was her chosen means of suicide

Daddy

Originally intended as the title-poem of the collection, 'Daddy' is an extraordinary outburst of hate directed against the poet's father. It is a cliché of psychology that a child will blame a dead parent passionately for the sense of loss the parent's death has brought, and Plath seems to have retained this emotion in full strength to her adulthood (in this respect it is perhaps significant that her father is still 'Daddy' to her). At the time she was writing the poem, the break-up of her marriage probably intensified the force of her feelings, in which her old resentment against her dead father was fuelled by her rage against her husband. Notice the repetition of the 'u' sound at the end of a line (do, shoe, Achoo, Jew, you, blue, and so on) which adds emphasis.

NOTES AND GLOSSARY:
Marble-heavy: like the statue of Colossus in the poem of the same name which also has her father for its theme
a head in the freakish Atlantic: an echo of 'Full Fathom Five', also in *The Colossus* collection
Ach, du: (*German*) ah, you
the Polish town: Otto Plath was born at Grabowa in the Polish Corridor, a territory often fought over
Polack: (*US*) a contemptuous nickname for a Pole
stuck in a barb wire snare: the German language became repellent to her because of the infamous concentration camps
Dachau, Auschwitz, Belsen: concentration camps
Tyrol . . . Vienna: Plath's maternal grandparents came from Austria
Luftwaffe, Panzer-man: the figure of her father becomes confused in her mind with images of the German air force and of the Panzer divisions, the German tank corps
You stand at the blackboard: in a photograph of Otto Plath taken in 1930
At twenty I tried to die: Sylvia Plath tried to commit suicide in 1953
a Meinkampf look: resembling Adolf Hitler (1889–1945), the German dictator and author of *Mein Kampf*

There's a stake in your fat black heart: the only way to prevent a vampire, the blood-sucking walking corpse of East European folklore, from rising from his grave is to put a stake through his heart

You're

Written during Sylvia Plath's first pregnancy, the poem is a string of loving, humorous, absurd descriptions of the baby she was carrying.

NOTES AND GLOSSARY:
Clownlike . . . like a fish: a description of the not yet fully developed baby curled in the foetal position
A common-sense/Thumbs-down on the dodo's mode: the human baby is the sensible, practical end-product of the developmental chain in which some species, like the dodo, were discarded
from the Fourth/Of July to All Fools' Day: the nine-month gestation period of the baby: Frieda was in fact born on All Fools' Day, 1 April
O high riser, my little loaf: an affectionate, homely image: the baby is growing like yeasty bread dough
Bent-backed Atlas: the curled foetus resembles the giant Atlas of classical mythology, bent low under the burden of the world he carries on his shoulders

Fever 103°

Written in October 1962 during a period of recurring high fever and flu, the poem consists of a series of feverish images and distorted sensations. The poet feels herself purified and made light by the high fever, light-headed, hypersensitive to touch, rising above her old selves.

NOTES AND GLOSSARY:
Cerberus: in Greek mythology the monstrous triple-headed dog who guarded the entrance to Hades, the underworld
Isadora's scarves: Isadora Duncan (1878–1927), American dancer, was strangled when the scarf she was wearing was caught in the wheel of her car
old whore petticoats: her discarded past

The Bee Meeting

The first of a series of beekeeping poems, it is a description of Plath's initiation by her neighbours into the craft of beekeeping. In spite of its homely, pastoral theme the poem is oddly sinister; the veiled villagers resemble members of some secret society, while Plath herself, dressed in white, appears to be the sacrificial victim of a secret ritual.

NOTES AND GLOSSARY:
scarves: floats like scarves
the bride flight,/The upflight of the murderess: if there are two queen bees in a hive, the younger one will kill the older queen and then fly off to mate
the magician's girl who does not flinch: a magician's, perhaps a knife-thrower's, assistant in a circus
Whose is that long white box: an image of a coffin, of death

The Arrival of the Bee Box

Beekeeping, which Sylvia Plath took up in June 1962, was to her a source of contentment, and this poem reflects this. It is interesting to remember that 'Insect Societies' and *Bumblebees* had been the titles of two of her father's publications. There are flashes of wit in this poem, and though on arrival the bee box reminds her of a coffin, a happy mood takes over, as she decides that the coffin must be that 'of a midget/Or a square baby'.

NOTES AND GLOSSARY:
I am not a Caesar: she cannot understand the bees' angry buzzing, 'like a Roman mob'
I have simply ordered a box of maniacs: no longer threatening, the box becomes a source of amusement
my moon suit and funeral veil: the beekeeper's protective clothing

Stings

With a beekeeper's help the poet is taking the honey out of the hives. She thinks of the worker bees, drudges like so many women. She herself had been one for years, submerged in domesticity and losing her 'strangeness', her poetic voice, but now she is free. Her husband is gone, and though she still thinks of him, she feels strong, vengeful, rising high.

NOTES AND GLOSSARY:

With excessive love I enamelled it: the Hugheses repainted old hives given to them

A third person is watching: she still feels the presence of her husband

scapegoat: the word has numerous nuances here: not only the person who takes on the blame, but also the one who has escaped, and the goat, with its strong sexual overtones

the square of white linen: Ted Hughes put a handkerchief on his head instead of a proper beekeeper's hat and was badly stung (letter to Mrs Plath of 15 June 1962)

thought death was worth it: the bee dies after it has delivered its sting

The mausoleum, the wax house: both the hive, and the house which had held Sylvia herself in domesticity

---

Wintering

Winter is an easy time for both bees and beekeepers. The honey has been extracted and is stored in jars. The bees now live on sugar, waiting for the spring. All the drones have been killed off, only the female bees survive. Winter is a woman's time, when she waits for the spring and for new life.

NOTES AND GLOSSARY:

the midwife's extractor: the tool for extracting honey from the combs, lent by the local midwife

Six cat's eyes: the jars of translucent yellow honey shine like cats' eyes

Tate and Lyle: the biggest sugar manufacturers in the UK

They have got rid of the men: the drones in a hive are killed in the autumn so that they do not have to be fed in winter

banking their fires: the corms of the gladioli have been covered over with earth but the plants will burst into colour in the spring

---

The Hanging Man

The title is taken from one of the tarot cards. Desperation drove him to hang himself. The prospect of sleepless nights and empty days brought him to suicide. In his place, God would have done the same. Some of the sensations described here can be traced back to Plath's own experiences of electric shock treatment.

Little Fugue

Another poem to her father. The yew tree blown by the wind seems to signal in dumbshow (as in 'The Moon and the Yew Tree' it seems to represent her dead father). The poet remembers a blind pianist on a ship. The thought of music brings to mind her father's voice, the amputation he had undergone, his death. In her memory her father's authoritative voice merges with that of her husband. Feeling threatened she finds refuge in daily tasks, in her baby.

NOTES AND GLOSSARY:

Grosse Fuge: *(German)* the great fugue. A fugue is a musical composition in which one part gives a theme which is then taken up by a second part ('answer') while the first part supplies an accompaniment

Such a dark funnel: her father absorbs her into himself (the image of a funnel appears also in 'Wuthering Heights' and 'Blackberrying' in *Crossing the Water*)

Dead men cry from it: Plath is understandably obsessed with her German/Austrian ancestry, with its burden of collective guilt for the horrors of the Second World War

You had one leg: the amputation which her father had undergone continued to haunt Sylvia Plath throughout her life

Years

One of Plath's last poems, full of a terrible impatience with living, thinking, with religion.

NOTES AND GLOSSARY:

the thoughts I turn on, like a Yogi: her bitter thoughts pierce her like the nails on which a yogi, a Hindu ascetic seeking to discipline himself through pain, lies

The piston in motion: the rhythm of passion (see also 'Getting There' where the piston stands for the human heart)

great Stasis: the moment of immobility before a great event

Dying to fly: dying on the Cross to rise to heaven, but also, in a colloquial phrase, eager to fly

The blood berries are themselves: the poet rejects religious symbolism, accepting objects for what they are

The Munich Mannequins

A scornful attack on barren beauty; the voice is that of a rejected wife and mother. Plath placed great weight on the ability to bear children, seeming to find in her motherhood a confirmation of her own worth. The snowy white background stresses the barrenness theme.

NOTES AND GLOSSARY:

Unloosing their moons ... to no purpose: a barren woman's menstruation is useless, cleansing the womb to no purpose

orange lollies on silver sticks: a grotesque image of the mannequins

Stolz: (*German*) pride

The snow has no voice: snow blankets all sounds

Totem

Another poem dealing with life in a series of fast-moving images. The engine is running fast, yet to no purpose. The butchery of animals goes on all the time. The individual dies, yet life continues – 'there is no terminus, only suitcases'.

NOTES AND GLOSSARY:

Smithfield: the London meat market, once a place of execution

eat it like Christ: a reference to the doctrine of transubstantiation, the belief that in Holy Communion the wafer becomes the body of Christ

Multiplied in the eyes of the flies: an oblique reference to the many-faceted eye of the fly

Paralytic

A paralysed man breathing through the iron lung lies motionless, watching. He remembers his wife and daughters still, but, stripped of all desires, he is at peace, as undemanding as a plant.

NOTES AND GLOSSARY:

My two/Dust bags: my lungs; the same image can be found in 'Apprehensions' in *Crossing the Water* ('Two grey, papery bags')

Mouth full of pearls: showing her teeth in a smile

Balloons

A happy poem addressed to the poet's small daughter, describing the pleasure the bright Christmas balloons had given them all.

NOTES AND GLOSSARY:
fat jug: a loving, amused description of a fat baby

Poppies in July

Written in summer 1962 when her marriage was breaking up. The red poppies evoke images of pain. If only the poet could feel pain, or sleep, if only the poppies could send her to sleep. The poem contrasts, presumably intentionally, with the later 'Poppies in November' in which the blazing colour is perceived as an unexpected gift.

NOTES AND GLOSSARY:
your opiates: opium is extracted from the unripe seeds of the white poppy

Kindness

A playfully sardonic acknowledgement of acts of kindness, expressed with a touch of sarcasm in colourful, pretty images: jewels, sugar crystals, butterflies, roses.

Contusion

Starting with a description of a bruise on the skin the poem continues with images of a whirlpool, an ominous crack in the wall, mirrors sheeted over – all portents of doom and death.

NOTES AND GLOSSARY:
The mirrors are sheeted: a covered mirror indicates a death in the house in some cultures

Edge

The subject of Plath's last poem is a woman who had killed herself. Suicide is her lasting achievement, she is at peace. The moon, cruel and unfeeling under her hood of bone, looks at her dispassionately, wearing black clouds like mourning.

NOTES AND GLOSSARY:
The illusion of a Greek necessity: to the Greeks suicide was not blameworthy, but sometimes the only honourable solution
Each dead child coiled: the memories of her children have gone with her
Pitcher of milk: in some cultures a saucer of milk is left out at night for the house snake, but the reader may remember also that Plath put out milk for her children before she killed herself

Words

A poem about words, a poet's working tool: their sound, their rhythm, the images they create. Words will live on even when the poet herself is dead.

Poems from *The Colossus and Other Poems*

The Colossus

The broken pieces of the huge statue of Colossus symbolise Plath's memories of her father which she is trying to piece together. The choice of the image is significant, as it implies her belief in the huge impact of her father, and especially of his death, on her entire being.

NOTES AND GLOSSARY:
Colossus: the statue of Colossus on Rhodes was one of the Seven Wonders of the ancient world. It was destroyed by earthquake in 22BC
To dredge the silt from your throat: to make you speak out of the past, to recreate a complete image
the Oresteia: the trilogy by Aeschylus (525–456BC) which has for its theme the murder of King Agamemnon by his wife Clytemnestra and her lover, and the revenge taken on them by Agamemnon's son Orestes. The tragedy is perhaps evoked as an oblique hint at a deep hostility between Sylvia Plath and her mother
Your fluted bones and acanthine hair: the image of a broken Corinthian column is also found in 'Manor Garden' in the same collection

All the Dead Dears

The women of her family are reaching out to the poet, the dead consuming the living like the mouse that gnawed the ankle of a woman in her coffin. The living go down to the dead as if into the sea.

NOTES AND GLOSSARY:

From the mercury-backed glass: through a mirror, by family resemblances

Where the daft father went down: her dead father is submerged by the waters of death (as in 'The Colossus' and in 'Full Fathom Five', both in this collection)

Full Fathom Five

The title uses the opening words of Ariel's song in Shakespeare's *The Tempest* (1.i.394) – 'Full fathom five thy father lies/Of his bones are coral made' – to indicate its subject. Like 'The Colossus' and 'All the Dead Dears' this poem too returns to the theme of Plath's dead father, and again there is the same equation of the sea with death.

NOTES AND GLOSSARY:

Durance: (*archaic*) durability

I would breathe water: the concluding line hints at death as the chosen option

The Disquieting Muses

The title comes from a painting by Giorgio de Chirico (1888–1978), an Italian painter of empty, dreamlike townscapes. The poem is a song of reproach directed against the poet's mother whom she blames for the terrors that lurk in her own mind. Like the bad fairies at a christening these terrors keep the daughter company while the mother remains ignorant of them. The poem weaves in memories of Plath's childhood, and echoes of fairy tales and old ballads ('And this is the kingdom you bore me to,/Mother, mother').

NOTES AND GLOSSARY:

heads like darning-eggs: this frightening picture recurs in 'Face Lift' in *Crossing the Water*

The Beekeeper's Daughter

Remembering that Otto Plath was an entomologist and author of a book on bumblebees the reader will readily identify the beekeeper's daughter with Sylvia Plath herself. The imagery is rich, heavy, overpowering: the speaker succumbs to her father. The emotional incest is brazen, unmistakable: 'Here is a queenship no mother can contest', 'Father, bridegroom'.

NOTES AND GLOSSARY:
The Golden Rain Tree: laburnum, *Goldregen* in German
anthers: part of the stamen of a flower that contains the pollen

Poems from *Crossing the Water*

Pheasant

A plea to a man (perhaps the poet's husband) not to kill a pheasant which has come to live nearby. The poet does not see the bird as some mystical spirit: she explains defensively that the creature's attraction lies simply in its beauty, in the sense of its fitting into the landscape. The poem does not rhyme, yet there are consistent consonance patterns (a rhyming not of syllables, but of the final consonants only): hill – at all, isn't – spirit – element.

NOTES AND GLOSSARY:
crosshatch: pattern of intersecting parallel lines, used for shading in drawings

Face Lift

Apparently inspired by the cosmetic operation which Plath's friend Dido Merwin had undergone, the poem is a little confusing, as the 'you' of the first three lines becomes the 'I' narrator of the poem. The poem plays with the idea that, having made her look younger, the operation has wiped out the later years of the woman's life. The rejuvenation is also linked with one of Plath's favourite themes, that of rebirth.

NOTES AND GLOSSARY:
the dewlapped lady/I watched settle, line by line, in my mirror: compare this image with the relentless 'Mirror' in

the same collection ('In me an old woman/Rises
toward her day after day')
sagged on a darning egg: the same image of a faceless figure recurs in
'The Disquieting Muses' in *The Colossus* ('with
heads like darning-eggs')

Parliament Hill Fields

After her miscarriage the poet walks on Parliament Hill in north
London, grieving for her lost baby.

NOTES AND GLOSSARY:
Your absence is inconspicuous: nobody misses the unborn child
your doll grip: the tiny baby's weak hold
Brood, rooted in their heaped losses: a startling metaphor of the trees
standing in heaps of fallen leaves
the old difficulties take me to wife: a reference to Plath's earlier
psychological problems which culminated in her
suicide attempt

Heavy Women

A poem in praise of fertility; in several poems Plath describes the joys
of motherhood, and expresses her abhorrence of barrenness.

NOTES AND GLOSSARY:
As Venus, pedestalled on a half-shell: an image probably inspired by
the famous painting *Birth of Venus* by Alessandro
Botticelli (1444–1510)
Mary-blue: blue is traditionally the Virgin Mary's colour
the straw,/The star, the wise gray men: three images drawn from the
scene of Christ's nativity

Among the Narcissi

The subject is the poet's Devon neighbour, Percy Key, recovering
after an operation for lung cancer. Images of sickness and death
contrast with the beauty of the flowers.

NOTES AND GLOSSARY:
bowing to some big thing: bowing to death
They bow and stand: like Percy, recovering from his serious
operation, the flowers bend and then stand
upright again

Poems from *Winter Trees*

Winter Trees

The 'otherworldliness' of trees is the subject of this poem expressing a yearning for calm detachment, absence of anger and pain, which Plath sees in trees: 'Knowing neither abortions nor bitchery'.

NOTES AND GLOSSARY:

Memories growing, ring on ring: a complex image which combines the rings seen on a cross-section of a tree trunk, each ring indicating a year's growth of wood, with the wedding ring of the bridal ceremony

they are Ledas: in Greek mythology Leda was the wife of King Tyndareos of Sparta. She was loved by Zeus in the shape of a swan. The relationship is seen here as asexual

these pietàs: a pietà is a statue or painting of the Virgin Mary embracing the dead body of Christ

Purdah

In this poem Plath is celebrating woman's liberation from man, the unleashing of the lioness (for this image see also 'Ariel') 'From the small jeweled/Doll' to a towering figure full of rage.

NOTES AND GLOSSARY:

Purdah: curtain screening women's rooms from the sight of strangers, used in India and Pakistan

The agonised/Side of green Adam, I: see 'It is Adam's side' in 'Getting There'

The shriek in the bath: perhaps a veiled reference to the murder of Jean Paul Marat (1743–93), one of the bloodthirsty extremists of the French Revolution. He was stabbed in his bath by Charlotte Corday (1768–93)

The Swarm

Its inspiration places this poem with the beekeeping poems of *Ariel*. Here the guns fired to make a swarm of bees settle turn the rural landscape into a battlefield of the Napoleonic wars. As the link between the two themes is purely aural – the sound of guns – the parallel may strike a reader as tenuous and unconvincing.

NOTES AND GLOSSARY:

The hump of Elba on your short back: Napoleon Bonaparte (1769–1821) spent his first exile (1814–15) on the island of Elba

a tod of ivy: a bush of ivy

bleb: a transparent blister, a bubble

Mary's Song

In the poet's imagination the Sunday roast turns into the fires that burned heretics and those of the gas ovens in the extermination camps in Poland during the Second World War. The cruelty of the world threatens to kill the golden child, in which the poet's own child merges with the infant Jesus.

NOTES AND GLOSSARY:

the cicatrix of Poland: Poland which suffered so much during the Second World War is seen as the scar of a wound

The Bell Jar: a general summary

Esther Greenwood, a college student, has won a fashion magazine contest, and is in New York for a month, all expenses paid, gaining editorial experience on the magazine. There are twelve winners altogether, all staying at the same hotel. Esther makes friends with the cynical Doreen who persuades her to skip some of the official parties. Doreen picks up a boyfriend, a disc jockey, and the two girls go to his apartment, but after a while Esther leaves and goes back to the hotel. Doreen returns in the morning, very drunk.

After an official luncheon given by a women's magazine for the contest winners all the girls fall ill with food poisoning, except Doreen who has again skipped lunch to be with her boyfriend. Esther is not enjoying herself in New York very much, and feels that she is wasting her opportunities. She is invited out to dinner by Constantin, a handsome UN interpreter and an acquaintance of her ex-boyfriend's mother. Esther hopes that Constantin will seduce her, but he does not seem very interested, and her depression deepens. The execution of the Rosenbergs, which takes place at this time, adds to her distress and confusion.

A lot of the time she is thinking of Buddy Willard, a boy she has known since childhood. He visited her at college when he came there to partner another girl, Joan, for a college dance. Esther began to see quite a lot of him afterwards and found it gratifying to be told that kissing her was a wonderful new experience for him. She was therefore shattered when Buddy told her that he had had an affair with a waitress. She now began to regard him as a hypocrite, and was going to break off their relationship when Buddy told her that he had contracted tuberculosis. She visited him at the sanatorium after Christmas, and Buddy gave her a skiing lesson which ended in her breaking her leg badly.

The relationship with Buddy is now obviously over, but Esther still thinks of him with resentment and would like to sleep with a man to pay Buddy back for what she regards as his hypocrisy. On her last evening in New York she again goes out with Doreen who has found another boyfriend. Esther's partner for the evening, Marco, proves to be a vicious woman-hater who nearly succeeds in raping her.

On her return from New York the next day Esther is bitterly disappointed to learn that she has not been accepted for the summer writing course on which she had set her heart, and will have to spend the vacation at home. Her mother works, and Esther is left on her own all day. She begins to suffer from insomnia, finds herself unable to read or write, and is taken to a psychiatrist.

The psychiatrist decides that Esther should undergo electric shock treatment which she finds deeply distressing and painful. She refuses to continue with the treatment and begins to think of suicide. She decides to cut her wrists but loses courage. Her courage fails her again when she tries to drown herself and then to hang herself.

In the end she takes a bottle of sleeping-pills from her mother's locked strongbox, crawls into a space under the floorboards of the house, and swallows the pills. She is found and rushed into hospital. She recovers physically, but her mental condition remains unstable.

A rich woman novelist, Mrs Philomena Guinea, on whose scholarship Esther had gone to college, interests herself in Esther's plight and offers to pay for the expenses of a cure in a private hospital for her.

At the hospital, under the care of a sympathetic young woman psychiatrist, Esther is beginning to recover. To her surprise a new patient at the hospital turns out to be Joan, the girl whose dancing partner Buddy Willard had been before he embarked on his relationship with Esther. Joan, however, now seems more interested in women than in men, something that Esther herself finds incomprehensible. Joan appears to be recovering well from her breakdown, and is allowed to live outside the hospital.

Esther's condition is also improving after a series of electric shock treatments, carried out this time with much more care and expertise, and far less shattering in their effect on her. She is allowed to go shopping in town on her own, and takes the opportunity to get herself fitted out with a contraceptive device.

She meets an attractive young professor in town, and goes to bed with him. The loss of her virginity causes her a heavy haemorrhage, and she goes for help to Joan. Joan accompanies her to a hospital where Esther is successfully treated. Though she tries to hide this from Joan, it seems likely that Joan has realised that Esther's bleeding was not menstrual but the result of sexual intercourse.

Joan's condition worsens, and finally she commits suicide. Esther comes to terms with her guilt about Joan's death, and prepares to meet the medical board which will decide whether she is well enough to go back to the outside world.

The Bell Jar: detailed summaries

Chapter 1

It is June 1953. Esther Greenwood is in New York, one of the twelve winners of a fashion magazine contest. The winners are staying at an expensive hotel for four weeks while working on the magazine. Esther likes only one of the girls, the cynical, amusing Doreen. On the way to an official party the two of them are picked up by a disc jockey, Lenny.

NOTES AND GLOSSARY:
The Rosenbergs: Ethel and Julius Rosenberg, American Communists, spied for the Soviet Union and were executed for treason in June 1953
Bloomingdale's: New York department store
pocketbook: (*US*) handbag
for the baby to play with: the only glimpse we are given of Esther's future
Sweetheart-of-Sigma-Chi: the most popular girl at college; US college fraternities (student societies) are named after letters of the Greek alphabet
B.H.Wragge: expensive make of women's dresses in the 1950s

Chapter 2

Esther and Doreen go with Lenny to his apartment. Lenny and Doreen dance, and they all drink. After a while Esther decides to go back to the hotel. In the morning Doreen returns, very drunk.

NOTES AND GLOSSARY:
a card: an eccentric, amusing person

grand: (*US slang*) a thousand dollars
the Sunflower State: Kansas
vamoosed: (*US slang*) left, departed

Chapter 3

The girls are at a special luncheon given in their honour by a women's magazine. Esther is enjoying the food but is depressed because that morning the editor to whom she had been assigned had berated her for not showing enough interest in her future. While listening to the editor, Esther was remembering how at college she had argued her way out of a compulsory science course.

NOTES AND GLOSSARY:
Howard Johnson's: chain of popular restaurants

Chapter 4

After the luncheon the girls are taken to a film premiere. Esther is feeling sick and so is Betsy, the girl next to her. They leave and go back to the hotel. Both are violently sick several times. It turns out that all the girls are ill, suffering from food poisoning after eating bad crabmeat at the luncheon. Only Doreen who missed the luncheon to be with Lenny is well.

NOTES AND GLOSSARY:
ptomaine: poisonous compound found in rotting meat

Chapter 5

Next morning Esther has a phone call from Constantin, an interpreter at the UN, who knows the mother of her ex-boyfriend, Buddy Willard. Esther has known Buddy from childhood, but he only became interested in her after she had gone to college. He was then at Yale, and came to Esther's college as the guest of another girl, Joan. Nevertheless it was Esther, not Joan, whom he invited to the Yale Junior Prom, a prestigious dance, which improved Esther's standing at college greatly.

NOTES AND GLOSSARY:
a poet who was also a doctor: the American poet William Carlos
Williams (1883–1963)
Russian short story writer: Anton Pavlovich Chekhov (1860–1904),
Russian story-writer and dramatist

Peter the Hermit: (*c*.1050–*c*.1115) French monk whose preaching inspired the disastrous 'Peasants' Crusade' against Turkish occupation of the Holy Land

Walter the Penniless: eleventh-century French knight who was jointly with Peter the Hermit the leader of the disorderly crusading armies

Sophomore Prom: dance for second-year students

Chapter 6

Buddy went on to Harvard to study medicine. When Esther visited him there, he showed her the dissecting room and the birth of a baby. Later, in his room, Buddy stripped naked to show himself to her. He also confessed to Esther that he had had an affair with a waitress while working at a hotel during the summer. Esther was furious, not from jealousy, but because Buddy had made her believe that he was sexually pure and that she alone was capable of rousing him to passion. She decided to put an end to the relationship, but then she learned that Buddy had contracted tuberculosis.

NOTES AND GLOSSARY:
a senior: (*US*) a fourth-year student

Chapter 7

Constantin arrives to show Esther round the UN building. While he is interpreting, Esther thinks of all the things she cannot do, and grows more and more depressed, as it seems to her that she is only good at passing exams. She looks to the future, imagining the various careers open to her.

Constantin takes her to a restaurant, and Esther likes him more and more. She decides to let him seduce her, to get her own back on Buddy. Constantin takes her back to his apartment, but does not make love to her, and she returns to her hotel. Her broken leg is aching.

NOTES AND GLOSSARY:
raking Mrs Willard over the coals: criticising Mrs Willard severely

Chapter 8

Lying in her hotel bed Esther remembers the time she broke her leg. It happened when she went to visit Buddy in the sanatorium where he was undergoing treatment for tuberculosis. Buddy proposed to her and would not listen when she told him that she did not want to marry at all. Later he gave her a skiing lesson. When he told her to ski down a steep slope she obediently did so, crashed and broke her leg in two places.

NOTES AND GLOSSARY:

P.A.S.: para-amino-salicylic acid, a drug used in the treatment of tuberculosis

---

Chapter 9

On the day of the Rosenbergs' execution Esther is talking to one of the girls, Hilda. Hilda is glad that the traitors are going to die, but Esther is distressed. During a photography session in the magazine offices she starts to cry and cannot stop. Doreen persuades her to accompany her to a party. The man who is to be Esther's partner, Marco, turns out to despise and hate all women. He treats Esther roughly and tries to rape her. She manages to fight him off and returns to the hotel. Sick at heart she throws her entire New York wardrobe from the sunroof of the hotel.

NOTES AND GLOSSARY:

dybbuk: in Jewish folklore the spirit of a dead person who enters the body of a living person
powder-room: (*US*) ladies' toilet
Tulsa, Biloxi, Teaneck, Coos Bay: towns in, respectively, Oklahoma, Mississippi, New Jersey, Oregon, representative of small-town America

---

Chapter 10

Esther returns home from New York to learn that she has not been accepted for a summer writing course, which is a bitter blow to her. As her mother works, Esther is alone in the house all day with nothing to do. First she tries to write a novel, then to work on her thesis, but is unable to concentrate on either. She cannot sleep, cannot read, has difficulty in writing, and her family doctor sends her to a psychiatrist.

NOTES AND GLOSSARY:

Barnard: Barnard College, a women's college in New York
riverrun, past Eve and Adam's . . .: the opening of James Joyce's (1882–1941) *Finnegans Wake* (1939)
Dylan Thomas: (1914–53), Welsh poet

| *Four Quartets*: | four poems by T. S. Eliot (1888–1965) |
| Beowulf: | Old English poem dating possibly from the eighth century |

Chapter 11

Esther's condition deteriorates: she cannot sleep, cannot write, does not want to change her clothes. The psychiatrist, Dr Gordon, does not seem sympathetic. He decides to send her for electric shock treatment. Esther begins to think of suicide, but returns home instead.

NOTES AND GLOSSARY:

WAC:	Women's Army Corps in the US army
WAVES:	Women's Reserve of the US navy
A.M.A.:	American Medical Association
the G.I. Bill:	popular name for the Servicemen's Readjustment Act, 1944, which guaranteed up to four years' free education to returning veterans
Big Dipper:	the Plough, a constellation of seven stars
Cassiopeia's Chair:	a constellation resembling a woman seated in a chair

Chapter 12

Esther has her first shock treatment and is shattered by it. She is now trying to find a way to kill herself. She gashes her leg with a razor blade, intending to lie in a warm bath and bleed to death, but she is afraid that her mother might find her still alive when she returns from work. Next she goes to the seashore near the little town where she lived as a child. On the way she talks to the guard at the prison there. She is planning to drown herself, but loses courage as she steps into the icy water.

NOTES AND GLOSSARY:

some old Roman philosopher or other: Seneca (*c*.5BC–AD65), condemned to death for taking part in a conspiracy against the emperor Nero, chose to die by opening his veins

Chapter 13

Esther goes to the seaside with her friend Jody, Jody's boyfriend and another boy, Cal. Cal and Esther swim together, and after Cal has

turned back Esther tries to drown herself, but fails. She had already
tried to hang herself but found the ceilings of the house too low. To
make herself think less of herself she signs on as a voluntary worker
at the local hospital, but this too is a failure. She goes to visit her
father's grave, something she has never done before, and cries
bitterly. Back home, as soon as her mother has left for work, Esther
breaks into her mother's strongbox, takes out a bottle of sleeping-
pills, and with the sleeping-pills and a glass of water crawls into a
space under the floorboards of the house. She swallows all the pills
and lies down to wait for death.

NOTES AND GLOSSARY:
this play where a young man finds out he has a brain disease: the
        Norwegian playwright Henrik Ibsen's (1828–
        1906) tragedy *Ghosts* (1891)
Chicken: (*US slang*) coward
They would be poor, too: during her years in England Sylvia Plath
        repeatedly expressed her admiration for the
        National Health Service which offers free medical
        care to all
the rainy armful of azaleas: Otto Plath's grave is on the Azalea Path
        of Winthrop cemetery, and there is a poem
        entitled 'Electra on Azalea Path' in her *Collected
        Poems* which has her father's death for its theme
breezeway: (*US*) roofed open-air passage connecting two
        buildings

Chapter 14

Esther is discovered in her hiding-place and taken to hospital. She
has injured her left eye and at first thinks she is blind, but soon
recovers her sight. She is transferred to a psychiatric ward of another
hospital. She hates the place and refuses to co-operate. The nurses
and orderlies dislike her.

NOTES AND GLOSSARY:
pompadour: hair combed back high above the forehead in a
        wave

Chapter 15

Mrs Philomena Guinea, Esther's rich benefactress, learnt of Esther's
suicide attempt and had her transferred to a private hospital at her
own expense. At the new hospital Esther watches the other women

patients and talks to her psychiatrist, Dr Nolan, a pleasant young woman whom she likes. A new patient arrives. This turns out to be Joan Gilling, the girl at Esther's college with whom Buddy Willard used to go out.

NOTES AND GLOSSARY:

the Charles: river on which Boston lies

the same glass bell jar: the image of the bell jar, a bell-shaped glass jar used in laboratories, is central to the book to which it gives its title: Esther feels as if she lived under glass, separated from other people and watched by them

Myrna Loy: (*b*.1905) American film actress of the thirties and forties, admired for her elegance and sophistication

OT: occupational therapy

I just grew fatter and fatter: there is an indirect reference to this effect of the insulin treatment in Chapter 3 ('With one exception I've been the same weight for ten years')

bang: (*US*) hair cut square across the brow

lobotomy: brain surgery, the cutting of the fibres between the frontal lobes of the brain and the thalamus, used in severe mental illness

Chapter 16

Joan tells Esther that she read about her suicide attempt at a time when she herself was consulting a psychiatrist, and that she had also tried to kill herself by cutting her wrists.

In the night Esther wakes up feeling strange and is told by the nurse that she is undergoing a reaction to the insulin treatment. Dr Nolan tells Esther that she is not to have any visitors. As Esther hates all visitors, including her mother, this pleases her.

NOTES AND GLOSSARY:

the Masons: Freemasons, a secret society

gymkhana: meeting for display of horseriding skills

out of the whole cloth: shamelessly, brazenly

Chapter 17

Esther is moved to the section of the hospital for patients who are on the way to recovery. Joan had preceded her there. One morning

Esther learns that she is to have electric shock treatment. She is terrified, but Dr Nolan promises to stay with her throughout, and they go to the treatment room together.

NOTES AND GLOSSARY:
do-re-mi: *(slang)* money

Chapter 18

When she wakes up after electrotherapy Esther feels at peace, free of fear: 'The bell jar hung, suspended'. After only five sessions she is regarded as well enough to go into town on her own. Joan, on the other hand, seems to have relapsed. She comes into Esther's room with a letter from Buddy asking if he could see her; Esther too has had a letter from him. Joan tells her that she prefers her to Buddy. That very morning Esther had found Joan in bed with another woman patient, and she wonders about lesbian relationships. On a shopping expedition in town she gets herself fitted out with a contraceptive device so that she can take a lover without fear of pregnancy.

NOTES AND GLOSSARY:
blind dates: *(US)* men friends or dance partners chosen for a girl by someone else
Schrafft's: patisserie and tearoom chain

Chapter 19

Joan has been allowed to live away from the hospital, sharing a flat with a nurse. Esther decides to find a lover to rid herself of her virginity so that she can be even with Buddy at last. At the library she meets Irwin, a young university professor, and goes back to his apartment with him. They make love, and Esther finds herself bleeding alarmingly. Irwin drives her to Joan's flat, and Joan takes her to a hospital to be attended to. A few days later Joan returns to the mental hospital because her condition has worsened again. Esther wonders if Joan's relapse was caused by her realisation that Esther's bleeding was not menstrual, but was really a very rare result of her loss of virginity. In the night Esther is woken up: Joan is missing. In the morning she is found dead: she has hanged herself.

Chapter 20

Esther is waiting for her interview with the medical board which will decide whether she is cured and can return to college and normal life.

Buddy has been to see her, wanting to ask her whether the mental illness and suicide attempts of both his girlfriends – Esther and Joan – have any connection with him. Esther is able to reassure him. She telephones Irwin to tell him to pay the hospital bill for emergency treatment after her haemorrhage.

She had been to Joan's funeral and felt strong enough to cope with the experience. She feels free now, and, though terrified, steps forward into the room for her medical interview.

NOTES AND GLOSSARY:

Grandma Moses: (1860–1961) highly successful self-taught primitive painter of New England landscapes of great charm

Part 3

Commentary

Sylvia Plath's poetry

Note: Unless stated otherwise, the poems mentioned below are from the *Ariel* volume.

Most of Sylvia Plath's poetry makes uncomfortable reading: we are constantly made aware of the huge emotions of rage, terror and despair that inspire Plath's verse and colour her imagery. It is not that her range is narrow but rather that the emotions she experiences affect her so deeply that they leave their mark on any subject. In one of Hans Christian Andersen's (1805–75) famous fairy tales, 'The Snow Queen', a tiny splinter of ice from the devil's magic mirror pierces the eye of the little boy Kay, and from that moment everything he sees appears to him ugly, mean or deformed. Sylvia Plath's vision is not ugly; on the contrary her deep awareness of beauty is unquestionable (see for instance 'Letter in November'); yet, however beautiful the images she sees, they arrange themselves in patterns of death and despair.

There are, of course, links between themes and imagery in any poetry, but in Plath's writing the strength of her themes not only dictates the images chosen to express them (as is the case with most poetry), but consistently transforms them. Red tulips become bleeding wounds ('Tulips'), a frosty window is 'glittering with dead breath' ('A Birthday Present'), the moon is a face with its mouth gaping in a grimace of despair ('The Moon and the Yew Tree'). In any discussion of her poetry, therefore, the themes that recur and dominate deserve the reader's attention before any other aspect of her work.

Themes

As we shall see, there are strong links between three of the recurring themes.

Death

Death entered Sylvia Plath's life early, with the death of her father when she was only eight years old. It was natural that she should have been deeply affected by such a shattering introduction to a phenomenon incomprehensible to a child in its enormity. Yet there was something in Plath's nature that responded to the idea of death with an abiding eagerness. Silent in her childhood (her mother kept the children from their father's funeral and suppressed her own grief), Plath's obsession with death spoke out in her adult poems.

In poems like 'Berck-Plage', 'Getting There', 'Edge', death is expressed in traditional terms: the pain, the loss, the dreadful distancing of the dead from the living. The accuracy of observation, for example in 'Berck-Plage', is explained by a chillingly honest note in Plath's diary, which records how, after a Devon neighbour, Percy Key, suffered a stroke, she first recoiled but then went to look at him, because something in her said, 'you must see this, you have never seen a stroke or a dead person'. The same detachment is employed in observing dead people as in examining dead animals ('Blue Moles', 'Medallion' in *The Colossus*).

There is, however, another vision of death in her poetry. Stripped of its awe-inspiring paraphernalia, this joking, slangy death figure loses nothing of its terror in 'Death & Co.'. Again in 'Totem' Plath rattles off a string of death images with a fearful levity, and in 'Lady Lazarus' death and resurrection become a fairground attraction. Here familiarity does indeed breed if not contempt then an almost companionable ease. Perhaps to a woman who had long played with the idea of suicide, death became almost a commonplace, a part of her vision of life.

Even where it is not the main theme of a poem, death is never far distant. In 'Sheep in Fog', 'Cut', 'Elm', 'Blackberrying' and 'I am Vertical' in *Crossing the Water*, 'All the Dead Dears' in *The Colossus*, and in others, death, if not the main subject, is the inspiration, the silent presence, the awaited end.

Rebirth
Naturally linked to the theme of death is that of rebirth. This is not the resurrection of Christian faith (Christianity plays only a small part in Plath's vision: the 'Mary-blue', discussed below in 'Images', is used more as a shorthand symbol of motherhood), but a personal rebirth, the rebuilding of a new life out of the ashes of the old one. It is a strengthening, invigorating act, a gathering of strength – for revenge, as in 'Lady Lazarus' or 'Stings', or for self-fulfilment, as in 'Ariel'. It can also be a purification, a spiritual renewal, as in the concluding line of 'Getting There', and, coming oddly after the vicious mockery, in 'Face Lift' (*Crossing the Water*). Beside the death theme in Plath's poetry rebirth appears somehow diminished, lacking the power, the conviction with which she could invest her hymns of mortality.

The father figure

A child of the post-Freudian age, who had undergone psychoanalysis, Sylvia Plath was quite aware of her Electra complex, her obsession with her father, and, inevitably, her hostility towards her mother as a rival. Her father's early death intensified her preoccupation with death, linking the two obsessions in her mind.

In the *Colossus* volume her dead father is a tragic godlike figure, the broken statue half-silted up, the floating drowned man with his hair spread out behind him ('The Colossus', 'Full Fathom Five' with its elegiac echoes of Shakespeare). The incestuous obsession is only obliquely hinted at, in a reference to the Oresteia in 'The Colossus'. The one poem with a direct reference to Electra in its title, 'Electra on Azalea Path', inspired by a visit to her father's grave, was omitted from the collection. Plath did include, however, 'The Beekeeper's Daughter' with its sensual images of flowers, and its shocking address to 'Father, bridegroom'.

Having named the *Colossus* volume after a poem on her father, Sylvia Plath nearly named her last publication *Daddy* instead of *Ariel*, after another poem about her father. 'Daddy', which recalls the child in its title, is a bold declaration of freedom from a life-long obsession at last. It is an extraordinary outburst of hate, excusable only if viewed as a tool of psychotherapy. From the black father figure, the dead man who retained his hold on her because he was dead, Otto Plath becomes a Nazi, a Jew killer, a black devil whom his daughter set up and painted black so that she would feel justified in rejecting him. The father figure merges with that of her husband, and both are rejected together ('If I've killed one man, I've killed two'). It seems that she could only find the strength to reject the old obsession when fired with a new rage. In 'Little Fugue' we find an assertion of the daughter's separate identity tenuously defined, along with a new, human figure of her father.

The mother

Given Sylvia Plath's obsession with her father, her hatred of her mother as a rival becomes inevitable. This attitude to her mother is, however, far from being a simple textbook case of an Electra complex. It is natural that she should resent her dependence on her mother which continued into adulthood and was both financial and emotional. What goes oddly with the smouldering resentment and the outbursts of vituperation in her poetry, is the tone of her letters home. We have all been guilty of editing reality for the benefit of our parents, whether this was to spare them pain or to stop their prying interference, but the gushing effusions in Plath's letters go well beyond the call of duty. The descriptions of the lovely meals she cooked, straight from *Ladies' Home Journal*, the naïve boasting of successful lion-hunting in London literary circles, speak clearly of an anxious desire for approval, for praise. The little girl who learnt to read so early and did so well at school later, stands there still, eager for the rewards of being good and clever. But this yearning squares uneasily with the reality of the situation. Sylvia Plath felt herself cheated out of her due share of love, by her father's death and by her mother's absence at work, and there is very little real warmth of affection in her letters to her mother.

Even so, the strength of her hatred will shock the reader. In her earlier poems in *The Colossus* – 'All the Dead Dears' and 'The Disquieting Muses' – there is resentment at the tug of family ties, to which in the latter poem she adds a note of bitter reproach – did she not inherit from her mother her disquieting muses, her three bad fairies? The closing lines of the poem:

> And this is the kingdom you bore me to,
> Mother, mother. But no frown of mine
> Will betray the company I keep.

offer the key to the two sides of Sylvia Plath's attitude to her mother, the resentment and resolve to blame, however unfairly, and the equally firm resolve to smile and deceive. Hence those jolly letters, written at the same time as the bitter poems. One of the poems in *The Colossus*, 'The Beekeeper's Daughter', already points forward to the vicious poems in *Ariel*, in that it puts the rivalry between mother and daughter into plain words: 'Here is a queenship no mother can contest'.

In *Ariel* this antagonism finds new forms; not just competing with her daughter for the father's love, here the mother is seen as destructive, relentlessly possessive ('Old barnacled umbilicus', 'Fat and red, a placenta' in 'Medusa', the cold moon face in 'The Moon and the Yew Tree', the love that will not let go in 'The Rival'). It seems that, as the father figure recedes, is exorcised, the full strength of the distraught daughter's hatred turns against her mother.

Motherhood
Whatever she felt about her own mother, Sylvia Plath found satisfaction and fulfilment in motherhood, epitomised in her poem 'Heavy Women' in *Crossing the Water*. One might almost say that motherhood was for her an affirmation of her own identity, a reassurance:

> You are the one
> Solid the spaces lean on, envious.

> 'Nick and the Candlestick'

52 · Commentary

These are my fingers, this my baby.

'Little Fugue'

She knows the pure enchantment of watching a baby, the amused tenderness of a mother: the new-born Frieda has been 'set . . . going like a fat gold watch' ('Morning Song'), little Nicholas 'sits/Back, fat jug' ('Balloons'). In 'You're' the images of the baby she is carrying are full of humour as well as affection ('O high-riser, my little loaf'), a far cry from the 'snail-nosed babies' in glass jars in 'Two Views of a Cadaver Room' from *The Colossus* and the stillborn babies with 'a piggy and a fishy air' in 'Stillborn' (*Crossing the Water*). In 'Morning Song' she sees herself in a warm, loving light, as she goes to her baby's cot at night, 'cow-heavy and floral/In [her] Victorian night-gown'. She envelops her child in the warmth of her love ('I have hung our cave with roses,/With soft rugs' – 'Nick and the Candlestick').

There is love which turns almost to awe in 'The Night Dances', and a fierce protectiveness in 'Mary's Song' (*Winter Trees*) for the 'golden child the world will kill and eat'. In 'Parliament Hill Fields' (*Crossing the Water*) there is pain as well as love for the baby she miscarried. The tiny baby is forgotten: 'Your absence is inconspicuous', its 'doll grip' too weak to maintain its hold.

Yet this love can stand at a distance, watching itself:

I'm no more your mother
Than the cloud that distills a mirror to reflect its own slow
Effacement at the wind's hand.

'Morning Song'

It appears to prepare itself for the final act of withdrawal, symbolised in 'Ariel'. As the woman-arrow flies into the sun, 'The child's cry/Melts in the wall', and is heard no more.

Different aspects of motherhood are presented in her radio play *Three Women* (published in *Winter Trees*). The three speakers are all women in a maternity ward, one the proud mother of a son, one a woman who has miscarried, and the third the mother of a baby daughter whom she is giving up for adoption. These separate voices of self-fulfilment, self-accusation, and rejection and guilt speak together of a human experience that was for Sylvia Plath, as for other women, self-defining.

Barrenness
Setting a high value on motherhood, Sylvia Plath abhorred barrenness. There is something disturbing in the virulence with which she attacks barren women. After the break-up of her marriage she labelled the women of her circle whom she no longer regarded as

friends, 'this set of barren women'. To her, barrenness is hard and cruel, like the moon in 'Elm', self-regarding and vain, like the 'Munich Mannequins'. The hostility becomes understandable, however, if we consider just how high a value she set on motherhood. For her, a childless woman was a threat, not just to her marriage, but, far more than that, a threat to the value that Plath placed on herself, and so had to be condemned with vehemence.

Feminism

This is the theme in Plath's work that has been examined most thoroughly. Certainly after her marriage, and especially after the birth of her children, she grew increasingly aware of the difficulty of simply finding the time to write. As early as May 1958 she wrote in her journal, 'Oh, only left to myself, what a poet I would flay myself into', and after the breakdown of her marriage she said in a letter to her mother (21 October 1962) that she was writing 'Terrific stuff, as if domesticity had choked me'. In her poem 'A Birthday Present' she offers an ironic picture of herself:

> Measuring the flour, cutting off the surplus,
> Adhering to rules, to rules, to rules.
> Is this the one for the annunciation?
> My God, what a laugh!

Similarly in 'Stings' she looks back, declaring:

> I am no drudge
> Though for years I have eaten dust
> And dried plates with my dense hair.

Resentment of the demands on her time made by domesticity is one aspect of her feminist image. Another is her hostility to and rejection of marriage and men. We find this hostility in 'The Applicant' with its venomous salesman's patter, in 'Purdah' (*Winter Trees*) where the 'small jeweled/Doll' of a man's imagination becomes the lioness that fights her way out of her cage, and in 'The Zoo Keeper's Wife' (*Crossing the Water*), which contrasts the husband's coarseness with his wife's sensitivity. In 'Wintering' there is an obvious equation of the drones in the hive with men, 'blunt, clumsy stumblers, the boors'.

Yet if these poems express dislike and revulsion from men, what are we to make of poems like 'Lesbos' (*Winter Trees*), 'Spinster' (*The Colossus*), 'Face Lift' and 'The Tour' (*Crossing the Water*), or 'Kindness', all poems about women and all full of spite or mockery? There is little feminine solidarity to be found there.

The conclusion, if one can be reached, is perhaps that Plath found it hard to fulfil all her chosen roles satisfactorily, perfectionist that she was, and that, ironically, the emotions that fuelled her poetry were grounded in that part of her life which made writing difficult. Her attacks on men, written at a time of distress, were attacks on her husband, and should be read in conjunction with other poems in which she turns with equal force on women.

Imagery

Sylvia Plath's vision is clear and precise, and her images have a vividness that is all her own. They are predominantly visual; indeed only rarely do we find an image that is based on an aural perception, such as the transformation of the gunshots, intended to bring a swarm of bees down to settle, into the sound of a Napoleonic battle in her poem 'The Swarm' (*Winter Trees*).

She likes sharp, bright colours: red – the colour of blood and therefore of life, a vivid green ('soft, delectable' – 'Letter in November'). Black is ominous, bringing back the dark figure of her dead father, evoking the picture of his amputated foot in a black boot ('Berck-Plage'). White is also a colour to be feared, the colour of bandages, of a hospital bed. In 'Moonrise' (*The Colossus*) it becomes the colour of putrefaction. Elsewhere too it may be the colour of death: in 'Berck-Plage' the dead man's nose rises above the sheets 'so whitely unbuffeted'; the newts and fish of the deadly cave of 'Nick and the Candlestick' are white.

Blue is to her a code colour: 'Mary-blue', the traditional blue of the Virgin Mary's cloak, becomes a symbol of motherhood. Her 'Heavy Women' in *Crossing the Water* await the birth, hooded by the dusk in 'Mary-blue'; in 'Widow' (*Crossing the Water*) the dead husband's soul hovers outside the window like 'blue Mary's angel'. In 'The Moon and the Yew Tree' the moon is the poet's mother, 'not sweet like Mary', and her blue garments hide bats and owls. Here the symbolism is reversed, but for the reversal to be effective the symbol must first be known for what it is.

There are other such symbols or coded images in Plath's poetry, a number of them associated with death. The sea, linked with the image of the dead, drowned father in 'All the Dead Dears' and 'Full Fathom Five' in *The Colossus*, and in 'A Life' in *Crossing the Water*, is one such symbol. In 'Suicide off Egg Rock' (*The Colossus*) the 'forgetful surf' offers peace after the noisy squalor of living, while in 'Blackberrying' (*Crossing the Water*) the path leading down to the sea ends in nothingness, in death, and in 'Berck-Plage' the entire seashore teems with images of disfiguration, horror and pain.

Another powerful symbolic image is the moon. Other poets'

inspiration, to Plath the moon stands for barrenness, negation of life. It is increasingly used in her later poetry, as she becomes more and more preoccupied with childbirth and childlessness, and as the mother figure, loveless to her, moves to the centre of the stage of her mind. In 'Elm' the moon is merciless and cruel, 'Diminished and flat', as after a mastectomy. In 'The Rival', possibly addressed to the poet's mother, the whole first stanza equates the rival with the moon, both leaving 'the same impression/Of something beautiful, but annihilating'. Both of them, significantly, borrow light but do not give out any, that is, they do not give out warmth or love. In 'Edge' the moon, under her 'hood of bone', looks at death calmly, unfeelingly. The consistency of meaning in this symbol is quite remarkable.

Another dark symbol, capable of more than one interpretation, is the mirror. It can mean death, as in 'Last Words' in *Crossing the Water* ('My mirror is clouding over'), and, obliquely, in 'All the Dead Dears' (*The Colossus*) in which the dead women of her family reach out to her in the mirror, and, again, in 'Contusion' with its sheeted mirrors in a house of mourning. In 'The Couriers' it merges with that other death symbol, the sea.

The mirror can also become a symbol of alienation: it is a reflection of the self, but the face that looks back from the mirror may be that of a stranger. This alienation is hinted at in 'Morning Song' with its image of a clouded mirror, in 'Mirror' (*Crossing the Water*), in 'The Burnt-out Spa' in *The Colossus*, and perhaps also in those faces changed by age in 'Face Lift' (*Crossing the Water*), and again in 'Mirror'.

Discussion of the symbolic images in Plath's poetry, however, should not obscure the vividness and immediacy of those of her images that are rooted not in her mind but in the world around her. In 'Morning Song' the crying baby's mouth 'opens clean as a cat's'; in 'Berck-Plage' the funeral is evoked with marvellous economy in 'Six round black hats in the grass and a lozenge of wood'. In 'Wuthering Heights' (*Crossing the Water*) the wind 'pours by' above valleys 'black as purses'. A simple phrase can invest everyday objects with a glittering terror: 'The smile of iceboxes annihilates me' ('An Appearance' in *Crossing the Water*). 'Two grey, papery bags' are the human lungs in 'Apprehensions' (*Crossing the Water*) and again in 'Paralytic' ('My two/Dust bags'). Such images may surprise or even shock us into recognition of their rightness.

Diction

Shock tactics are an essential part of Sylvia Plath's technique, especially in her later poems. Her unexpected use of colloquialisms

('I do it so it feels like hell' – 'Lady Lazarus'; 'Somebody's done for' – 'Death & Co.'; 'Who do you think you are' – 'Medusa') is intended to shock.

We are told that Sylvia Plath first wrote her poems with a thesaurus on her lap and that she used it frequently, searching for the right word. Written with care for the right words, such poems were intended to be read slowly, tracing the images in their complex patterns. The effect was cerebral or visual, as were most of the images. In later years Plath gained enough confidence to abandon her thesaurus. She also changed her method of writing, reading the poems aloud to herself as she wrote them. She gave several poetry readings on the BBC, and in a broadcast interview commented that her work was written for the ear rather than the eye.

This change of aim and technique meant a considerable change in the nature of her verse. The poems for which she is best known – 'Lady Lazarus', 'Daddy' and 'Ariel' – and a number of others, all have a colloquial quality, sometimes a slanginess of diction, faster rhythms, approaching patter song at times, and a conciseness that is as demanding as the carefully built poems of her earlier years.

She uses half-rhyme, assonance, repetition, occasionally (and irregularly) rhyme to compel the reader's/listener's attention. She can be strident, terrifying in her rattling speed (as in 'The Applicant', in 'Ariel', and in the abusive outburst in 'Daddy'). Equally she can wring our hearts with one simple, quiet sentence: 'Love, love, my season' ('The Couriers'); 'The box is only temporary' ('The Arrival of the Bee Box'). Her poetic imagination may be predominantly visual, but she has learnt well how to speak directly to her readers.

The Bell Jar

Structure and technique

The Bell Jar begins abruptly, with an indirect announcement of the date when the story begins – June 1953, when the Communist spies Ethel and Julius Rosenberg were executed. The first two chapters tell us how Esther came to be in New York, and describe some of her fellow-winners, as well as an escapade in which one of them, Doreen, involves Esther.

Chapters 3–4 are still located in New York, though Chapter 3 ends with a lengthy flashback to Esther at college. Chapters 5–6 tell of Esther's involvement with Buddy Willard, and her reasons for wishing to end the relationship. Though Chapter 5 begins in New

York, both chapters have a college background – first Esther's college, then Yale and Harvard where Buddy continues his medical studies.

Chapter 7 returns to New York, but Chapter 8 is another flashback, to the sanatorium in the Adirondacks where Buddy is being treated for tuberculosis. From Chapter 9 onward the narrative adopts a straightforward chronological form, accompanying Esther through the stages of her breakdown which leads to her suicide attempt and ends with her recovery in hospital.

Basically, then, this is a straightforward story of Esther Greenwood's breakdown and her recovery. It starts in June 1953 and covers the whole of that summer, the following autumn and winter, ending not long after Christmas, in January 1954 (exactly the chronology of Sylvia Plath's own breakdown and recovery).

The story diverges from its chronological order three times: first with the flashback in Chapter 3, used to show the parallel in Esther's handling of her magazine boss and her Class Dean at college. The longest flashback takes up Chapters 5 and 6, and tells of Esther's relationship with Buddy. This subject is taken up again in the last flashback in Chapter 8. There are no more flashbacks after this, and the narrative moves forward chronologically.

We may wonder why the flashback was used at all. An obvious reason for its use is economy: instead of lengthily recounting Esther's year at college, followed by her stay in New York, her return home, her breakdown, her suicide attempt and her recovery, the author is able to start her story at the exciting point of the heroine's stay in New York, concentrating on the months before her breakdown – when the signs of mental distress were becoming obvious – and so heightening the dramatic effect of the story. The reader, trained by cinema-going to recognise a flashback and pick up the thread of the main story afterwards, will accept it for what it is – an explanatory aside, filling in the gaps in the background. The only surprising aspect of its use is how sparingly it has been used – probably because its purpose was simply to explain the affair of Buddy and the reasons for Esther's determination to gain sexual experience (though these same reasons may strike some readers as not entirely convincing). Once this has been done, the story stays with the harrowing account of Esther's breakdown.

Another narrative technique gained from the cinema is the abrupt switch of location. The homeward journey in Chapter 10 starts with 'The face in the mirror looked like a sick Indian', bringing in an element of surprise and excitement. Chapters 9 and 13 both begin with similarly macabre snatches of dialogue ('I am so glad they're going to die' – Hilda on the Rosenbergs in Chapter 9; 'Of course his mother killed him' – Cal on Mrs Alving in Ibsen's *Ghosts* in Chapter 13). Chapter 14 begins the account of Esther regaining consciousness with 'It was completely dark'. All these brief statements are effective because of their terseness.

The two techniques merge in the handling of Esther's brief encounter with Irwin. With no preliminaries and no explanations, the account begins with Esther complaining of the pain caused by the breaking of the hymen during sexual intercourse. In what might be called a mini-flashback Esther then describes her first meeting with Irwin, leads up to the defloration scene, and picks up the thread with a repetition of her plaintive remark. There seems little doubt that the scene is described in this way to make the most of its melodramatic quality.

Though the plot is chronological except for the flashbacks, the author quite deliberately avoids a continuous narrative in favour of separate short scenes and incidents which follow one another in time, but with no linkage. This form of narrative becomes more and more marked in the course of the novel, the nightmarish parade of disjointed incidents paralleling the confusion in Esther's mind, until the last chapter, when Esther neatly tidies up the loose ends of her tale, quite in the manner of a Victorian novelist. Order is restored, again mirroring the restored order in Esther's mind.

Language and style

Plath's narrative style is plain and colloquial, with a marked preference for short sentences. The poetic images which she uses sparingly are all the more effective for this:

> the countryside . . . turned us a bleaker shoulder . . .
>
> (Chapter 8)
>
> The great, grey eye of the sky looked back at me . . .
>
> (Chapter 8)
>
> the motherly breath of the suburbs enfolded me.
>
> (Chapter 10)
>
> her mouth blooming out of the quiet vase of her body like the bud of a rose.
>
> (Chapter 15)
>
> I . . . listened to the old brag of my heart. I am, I am, I am.
>
> (Chapter 20)

The same plainness of style marks the dialogue. Its colloquialisms, its use of slang are restrained: the author does not rely on them to convince the reader that her characters are living people.

Surprisingly for a novel on such a distressing subject there is a good deal of humour, of a dry, mocking kind: the girls in their taxis are 'like a wedding party with nothing but bridesmaids' (Chapter 1); (of a young baby) 'for all I knew it could talk a blue streak and had twenty teeth behind its pursed, pink lips' (Chapter 18).

What poetic images there are in the novel grow out of Plath's eagerness to record what she has seen and experienced so greedily, like Esther herself: 'If there was a road accident . . . or a baby pickled in a laboratory jar . . . I'd stop and look so hard I never forgot it' (Chapter 1). However plain the words, they still describe a world made anew by a poet's imagination.

There are other images in the novel, not transcriptions of things seen into vivid pictures, but symbols, images that have a special inner meaning. Foremost among them is of course the image of the bell jar, the bell-shaped glass jar used in research laboratories. In Plath's novel it becomes the symbol of alienation, of the invisible barrier that separates Esther from other people during her illness, imprisoning her in her misery. It lifts and hangs suspended over her head after the successful ECT treatment (Chapter 18), but even when she is cured she wonders if the bell jar 'with its stifling distortions' will not descend on her again. There is a link – made explicit in Chapter 20 – between this symbol of madness and the dead babies in glass jars which Plath herself, like Esther, had seen at Harvard medical school, and which affected her deeply.

There are other symbols in the novel, none used repeatedly, and all representing life: the famous picture of the fig tree with luscious figs representing different choices for the future (Chapter 7); the lovely rug made by Mrs Willard and trodden underfoot like her whole life (Chapter 7); Esther's life stretching ahead of her like the telephone poles along a road (but they stop at the nineteenth, the break symbolising the idea of suicide which is forming in Esther's mind – Chapter 10). The readers of Sylvia Plath's poetry will notice the absence here of the symbols so characteristic of her poems: the sea, the moon and the mirror, which are here visual pictures, not symbols with a private meaning.

Themes

Several themes may be traced in the novel, similar to Plath's poetry, though they may be treated differently.

Death
Obviously death must play a part in a novel dealing with a suicide attempt. In keeping with the jaunty, flippant style of the novel,

however, death is treated briskly, a problem to be solved. There is almost a touch of farce in the accounts of Esther's ˙ ˙ unsuccessful suicide attempts. Characteristically, Dodo Conway's station waggon is described as 'the dead spit of a hearse' (Chapter 12).

Only the execution of the Rosenbergs, which had contributed to Esther's breakdown, introduces a sombre note, seeming to fore-shadow for Esther her ECT treatment as she wonders what it must be like to be 'burned alive all along your nerves'.

In the second half of the novel we grow aware of a change. Esther's visit to her father's grave, with its coded reference to Azalea Path in Winthrop cemetery where Plath's own father is buried ('the rainy armful of azaleas' – Chapter 13), speaks of grief, of the pathos of dying, symbolised by the miserable, cheap, neglected graves. Esther's nearly successful suicide attempt which follows is no longer to be treated as a laughing matter.

With Joan's suicide and her funeral, death becomes truly a reality, no longer a joke, and it is a measure of Esther's recovery that she now sees it as real.

Feminism
The image of the fig tree in Chapter 7, often quoted to support the view of Sylvia Plath as a feminist, is all about choices. If we read it carefully we find that the choice is not simply between marriage and motherhood on the one side, and a career on the other. Marriage and children is one choice, but there are several others – poet, academic, magazine editor – and each of these will exclude the others. If Esther chooses to be an editor she cannot be a professor any more than she can be (or rather, could be, in the 1950s) a wife and mother.

Far more pertinent to the view that Plath saw marriage as an obstruction to artistic fulfilment is the symbolic rug made by Mrs Willard, significantly out of the scraps of her husband's suits, which was used as a kitchen mat and soon grew dirty and dull. Certainly Buddy's expectations of his future wife did not include her writing poetry, but then Plath makes it pretty clear that neither she nor Esther sees him as either intelligent or sensitive, and his views on marriage are all of a piece with his character. That his view of marriage as a career excluding all others was shared by women as well is demonstrated by the don at Esther's college; 'But what about your *career*?' she cries on hearing that Esther considers marriage a possibility.

One aspect of the differences in the treatment which society dished out to young men and women is the high value placed on a girl's virginity, and here Esther's resentment of the unfairness of this double standard is very clear. After all, most of the time she is anxious to shed her virginity just to get even with Buddy for his affair with the waitress. She declares that it is his hypocrisy in pretending to be sexually innocent that angers her, but her motives obviously include a wish to level out the differences, to be even.

Unfashionable today is Esther's intolerance of lesbians. She harshly rejects Joan's advances, and only when gently rebuked by Dr Nolan does she accept that a relationship between two women might offer them a tenderness lacking in a heterosexual love affair.

To sum up then, Sylvia Plath – speaking through Esther – resents certain aspects of the society she lives in, but is unable to construct a radically different alternative for herself. Her significance for the women's movement lies in the fact that she did question the attitudes and conventions of her time at all, ten years and more before the feminist movement first made itself heard.

Characters

Esther Greenwood
Inevitably most readers will wonder how much of Sylvia Plath there is in Esther Greenwood. Anyone who has read a biography of the author will be struck by the number of close parallels between Plath's own life and that of her heroine, testifying to her remarkable recall of events that had taken place nearly eight years before. The conclusion may be drawn that Esther is Sylvia Plath as she saw herself or as she wished to be seen by others.

Esther is very bright, witty, well read, a hard-working scholarship student. Pretty but not beautiful, she is deeply unsure of her ability to attract men, vital for her success in college society. To reassure herself on this all-important point she will welcome the overtures of young men who are evidently her inferiors intellectually, and who bore her. Because of her anxiety to be a success with men, she has few close friends of her own sex (in her first year at college she has only one friend, Jody). She likes Doreen, is attracted by her cynicism and impressed by her recklessness. She sees Doreen as much too attractive and sophisticated to be competed with at all, and therefore somehow easy to be with.

There is a noticeable lack of warmth in most of Esther's relationships. She dislikes her mother, finding her oppressive and too demanding in her expectations. She hardly speaks of her father, though the scene at his grave in Chapter 13 shows how shattered she had been by his death. Her brother is mentioned only briefly. Her relationship with Buddy seems grounded in her desire to have an enviable boyfriend rather than in any affection. Even when not isolated from other people by her 'bell jar' she appears distant, an observer taking notes, collecting material for her writing.

Some change is effected in her by Joan's death. Though she did not like Joan and found her advances distasteful, Joan's death – a successful suicide – seems to shatter Esther's detachment and thus contributes to her recovery.

Her enjoyment of food (demonstrated by her comic greed at the *Ladies' Day* luncheon) is frank and endearing, and may be seen as a symbol of her greediness for experience. Like Sylvia Plath herself, Esther observes and experiences eagerly, though always with a writer's awareness of her experiences as good copy.

Mrs Greenwood
When examining the character of Mrs Greenwood we must remember that *The Bell Jar* is an 'I' novel, and that all the characters are seen through Esther's eyes. Therefore all descriptions of other people serve a dual purpose: not only to make us see these people but also to make us aware of Esther's reaction to them (and thereby deepen our understanding of her). To Esther her mother is a tiresome conventional woman who annoys her daughter by always maintaining an air of determined cheerfulness and sweet reasonableness. (Her daughter never forgave her for treating her husband's death in this way).

Mrs Greenwood refuses to accept her daughter's mental illness ('I knew my baby was not like that' – Chapter 12), though she knows instinctively that her daughter is thinking of throwing herself into the river during the drive to the private hospital (Chapter 15). She has no real insight into her admittedly difficult daughter's mind. Her repeatedly expressed worry about the cost of Esther's treatment (understandable in the light of the family's finances) has the effect of heightening Esther's terror of being left, forgotten, in a state asylum. Her gift of roses on Esther's birthday shows her failure to understand her daughter's infatuation with death, not with birth and life. Briefly, she is a well-meaning, conventional woman, and it is her misfortune, as well as Esther's, that her daughter is the girl she is. The mother's absence at work, necessary as it was, probably contributed to the lack of affection in the mother/daughter relationship, as well as in Esther's relations with people outside her family.

Buddy Willard
Buddy, a fictionalised portrait of Sylvia Plath's boyfriend Dick Norton, is tall, conventionally handsome, a student first at Yale and then at Harvard; altogether the dream escort for a girl at a women's college. He is, however, a complete philistine who mocks Esther's

passion for literature. There is no real understanding between them, and no real love either. To her he is purely a social asset, and presumably her value to him is the same. It is never made clear why Buddy chose Esther for his girlfriend; the reader remains as puzzled as Esther herself.

It is obvious that Buddy is conceited and not particularly intelligent. In fact he is quite insufferable in his early years at college. Only during his last meeting with Esther (Chapter 20) does Buddy appear in a different light: his conceit has been shattered by his serious illness and by the rebuffs which he has met with from both Joan and Esther. Buddy now appears 'grave, even tentative', 'a man who often does not get what he wants'.

Joan Gilling

Outwardly Joan is quite different from Esther. A large, horsy girl with great pebble-like eyes, showing her big teeth in a broad smile, she seems the image of healthy normality. Yet she has had a breakdown, and once in the hospital realises that she is not attracted to men, has a lesbian relationship with one of the patients and shows that she is attracted to Esther.

Her role in the novel is a curious one. Esther remarks that she and Joan 'were close enough so that [Joan's] thoughts and feelings seemed a wry, black image of [her] own' (Chapter 18). Joan had been Buddy's girlfriend first; she, however, followed Esther in trying to kill herself; she followed her also to the hospital; she turned down Buddy, as did Esther, too: and, finally, succeeded where Esther had failed – in killing herself.

The parallels are too marked to be accidental, and as, unusually (for *The Bell Jar* is closely modelled on Plath's own life), there was no real-life model for Joan, the author must have invented her for a purpose. She is Esther's alter ego, an image of what she might have become, and for that reason she is ultimately granted her creator's rare sympathy and compassion.

The Bell Jar as autobiography

The Bell Jar is a fictionalised autobiography. There is nothing particularly unusual in that: there are many examples of this genre, for instance Charles Dickens's (1812–70) *David Copperfield* (1850) or James Joyce's (1882–1941) *A Portrait of the Artist as a Young Man* (1916). What is unusual is the high degree to which *The Bell Jar* reflects the events in Sylvia Plath's own life during the period of summer and autumn 1953 and early 1954, and, in flashbacks, in 1950–1. Her own distress at the execution of the Rosenbergs provides the opening of the novel. Her own experiences in New York as guest editor on *Mademoiselle* magazine are recounted right down to an attack of food poisoning, a blind date with a Peruvian which ended in a near-rape, and her throwing her New York wardrobe out of the hotel window. Even small details, like the colour of the dirndl skirt and the style of the blouse which she had to borrow from one of the other girls after discarding her own wardrobe so dramatically, are the same.

The dejection of that summer which culminated in her suicide attempt is again accurately recounted in the novel, as is her stay in a private hospital, paid for by Mrs Prouty, and her recovery under a sympathetic woman psychiatrist. As was mentioned in the 'Characters' section above, the character of Joan Gilling is the only one of any importance in the novel which does not seem to be based on a real-life person (though Joan's suicide had a real-life counterpart in the suicide of a Smith freshman student in 1957 when Plath was back at Smith as a teacher).

The closeness of the novel to the novelist's own life is certainly surprising. Equally surprising is the skill with which she shaped the events of her own life into the compact form of *The Bell Jar*. Her use of the flashback to fill in the background enables her to contain the action within the space of a few crucial months, so maintaining the jerky, fast pace of the novel. Rather less surprising is her decision to publish it under a pseudonym, given the ease with which the originals of the characters in the novel could be identified.

A translation of raw personal experiences into a fictionalised narrative can be achieved successfully, then, while retaining recognisable features of the original experiences. These same experiences were the inspiration of Plath's poetry as well, but there are few easily recognisable parallels to be found there. When reading a poem such as 'Two Views of a Cadaver Room' (*The Colossus*), we may remember the visit to the dissecting room with Dick Norton, also described in Chapter 6 of *The Bell Jar*, but such a clear presentation of a real-life experience is rare in Plath's verse. A visit with Ted Hughes to Berck-Plage in 1961 inspired the eponymous long poem with its images of disfigurement and death, but in the poem the seaside sanatoria of Berck-Plage merge with the memories of the death and funeral of a Devon neighbour. These are experiences, not 'recollected in tranquillity', but distilled and enlarged beyond the events that inspired them.

Part 4

Hints for study

Studying *The Bell Jar*

Though these Notes deal with Plath's verse first, and discuss her poetry at greater length, it might be useful for you to begin your study of her work by reading *The Bell Jar*. If you have not been able to get hold of a biography of the poet, you will find her novel particularly helpful. It illuminates a painful period in the author's life which inevitably shaped the way in which she saw herself and the world in which she lived. The novel also spotlights some of the preoccupations that determined the ideas and emotions expressed in her verse: death, the vacancy left in her life by her father's death, her dislike of her mother, her ambiguous feelings about marriage and children and about sexual relationships.

Read the novel right through first, for pleasure. Though much of it is distressing, it is a surprisingly amusing, witty book, easy to read.

After your first reading, go through the novel again, slowly, chapter by chapter. Make notes on each chapter, summing up briefly what is happening; include the details of the flashbacks, of the changes of location (you will find these notes useful when considering the structure of the novel).

During your first reading you will have noticed some of Esther's preoccupations. Now is the time to identify them in your mind: death, virginity, marriage, parents, and so on. Make a list of the themes that interest you before you embark on your second reading, and then write down under each heading the chapters (with page numbers) in which a particular theme occurs in the novel.

Pay attention to Plath's style: the conciseness, the brevity of the sentences, the flashes of humour, the simple, realistic dialogue. Pay special attention to the images, notice how they stand out against the simple style. Look out for echoes of Plath's poems in the novel, particularly if you are interested in parallels between her novel and her verse.

This is the time to take down a few quotations, but make sure that they will be useful to you. By now you should have some idea of the aspects of the novel on which you would like to concentrate, and the quotations you select for memorising should be relevant to any arguments you put forward in an essay or examination question.

You should know by now that you must quote accurately, if

possible with a chapter reference. If, working under stressful conditions, you find yourself unsure of the exact wording of a quotation, describe it rather than risk misquoting. For instance, if you had intended to quote the description of Miss Norris in Chapter 15 and find you cannot remember it accurately, refer instead to the comparison of her thin body to a vase, with her round silent mouth resembling a rosebud.

Having completed your notes on *The Bell Jar*, read them through carefully. Try to work out which aspects of Plath's novel are likely to be the subject of examination questions. If you are able to consult examination papers from previous years, this will help you to make a fairly accurate educated guess as to the form these questions could take. (There is a list of suggested examination questions on Sylvia Plath's work later in these Notes, which you might use.)

If it is at all possible, choose a question which really interests you. You are likely to produce a much better answer if you find the subject genuinely interesting.

You should have checked by now how long the examination for which you are working is going to be, and how many questions you will be expected to answer. Work out how much time you can allow for each question, but remember to allow extra time, first for deciding on the questions you will answer, and, at the end, for reading over your answers. When working under pressure it is only too easy to leave out words or allow spelling errors to creep in.

Now you can start testing yourself in answering a question. Sit down (with an alarm clock by you if you like), and start writing.

First write down a brief outline of your argument: an introduction which will indicate the line your answer will take, then the main part which states your argument in detail, supporting it with references to the text of the novel, and quotations if possible. Lastly a summary, which recapitulates your argument. Test your planned answer against the question to make sure you have understood it correctly and are answering it. You may agree or disagree with the question, but you must answer it, your answer must be relevant. Do not be tempted to stray; you may find, as you write, that new, interesting ideas occur to you. Test them against the wording of the question; however stimulating a new line of thought may appear, it is useless if it is irrelevant. When you have finished, remember to read over your answer carefully. If you find that you have run out of time, try to identify the reasons: was your answer too long or have you been too ambitious, pursuing new lines of thought and forgetting about the time limit? (If this should happen to you during the examination, put a brief note at the end, showing how you had intended to develop your argument and what would have been your conclusions.)

Studying Plath's poetry

Discussing Sylvia Plath's novel is a fairly straightforward proposition. Her poetry, however, is quite a different matter, and your approach should be different. The first thing to remember is that there is no single correct interpretation of most of her verse. If you have read more than one critical work on her poetry, you will have noticed that the critics do not always agree on the meaning of a particular poem. We all interpret poetry in the light of our own experiences: the images and symbols will mean something slightly different to each of us. It is only the consistent use of an image that will alert the reader to its special meaning in a poet's personal vision. Such symbols are signposts in a poet's landscape, but there are no reliable guides that will map out the terrain in detail. You should bear this in mind when studying Plath's poetry. As there is no single correct interpretation, you should not be afraid to offer your own reading of a poem, as long as it is honestly thought out and based on a careful study of her verse.

Even if you are planning to study only one of her collections in detail, you will find it profitable as well as interesting to read some of her other works as well. Selected poems from her other books, in addition to *Ariel*, are discussed in Part 2 above. In Part 3 you will notice references to poems from all her collections and you may observe how her poems complement and illuminate each other across the collections. There is a list of her published works in Part 5, 'Suggestions for further reading', should you decide to widen your knowledge of Plath's verse.

By all means begin by reading a collection such as *Ariel* straight through, making notes of your impressions. Quite often such first impressions, fresh and uninfluenced by any study of critical works, will prove valuable.

Follow the first reading of your chosen volume by a careful second reading, poem by poem, making notes on each poem. Such notes should include your interpretation of the poem, plus notes on what struck you particularly about its themes, images and language. You might like to think about grouping the poems according to main themes: such groups of the poems in *Ariel* might include poems on children, landscape poems, poems inspired by Plath's complex memories of her father and her feelings about her mother, death poems, poems on women, on her marriage and her husband, the so-called 'beekeeping' poems, and so on. Such classification may strike you as a sterile exercise, but you will find that trying to decide which poems belong together can help you to understand them.

You should now find that your reactions to individual poems are beginning to crystallise, your preferences are becoming clearer. This is the time to decide on which groups of poems you would like to concentrate. Do not limit yourself to one group of poems only; make sure that your choice is wide enough to give you a grasp of Plath's range and techniques. (That is to say, for instance, do not pick out just the poems about her father, however well known they are. There is more to Plath's verse than an Electra complex.)

Analyse the poems you have chosen for special study with care, line by line, image by image. You will notice parallels, recurrent symbols, hints of her own life experiences, lines that throw light from one poem to another. Make a note of them, choosing quotations to memorise and use in your interpretations and comments.

Read over your notes on each group. You should find enough material to shape your notes into an essay. Test yourself again by writing the essay within a time limit, as during an examination. (Follow the hints on essay writing given above in the discussion of *The Bell Jar*.)

Two points are perhaps worth emphasising. First, do not be afraid of offering your own interpretation of the poems even if you can quote no literary authority to back you. Plath's vision is a deeply personal one, and many words and symbols have a particular meaning for her, which no one else can entirely share. That being so, however, all readers can and should use their own emotions and experiences to find their own meaning for a poem.

Second, though Sylvia Plath's poetry is difficult, and the task of interpreting it may seem daunting, it can be enjoyable. There is great pleasure to be gained from using one's mind and heart to find the meaning of a complex poem, and much satisfaction in that sudden flash of understanding that comes as the meaning becomes clearer. There is also great delight in the wealth of startling and beautiful images employed by the poet in expressing her feelings and thoughts.

Specimen questions

(1) *The Bell Jar* is largely autobiographical. Can it still be regarded as a novel?

(2) 'She wanted her novel to speak for the lives of countless women' (Linda W. Wagner, *Sylvia Plath*). Do you agree with this view of *The Bell Jar*?

(3) Esther's suicide attempt might be described as the turning-point of the novel. Illustrate (or refute) this view by reference to the structure and style of the novel.

(4) 'She created a language for herself that was utterly and startlingly original' (John Carey, *Sunday Times*, 5 November 1989). Discuss.

(5) Consider Plath's use of the moon as a metaphor.

(6) Assess Plath's view of women as expressed in her poetry.
(7) Choose one of the following themes and discuss Plath's treatment of it in *Ariel*: (a) motherhood and barrenness; (b) marriage; (c) death.
(8) Can Plath's poetry be understood with no knowledge of her life?
(9) Contrast the father figure in 'The Colossus' and in 'Daddy'.
(10) Take any two of Plath's nature poems and discuss the treatment of nature in both as a reflection of the poet's mood.

Specimen answer

(4) 'She created a language for herself that was utterly and startlingly original' (John Carey, *Sunday Times*, 5 November 1989). Discuss.

At first glance this seems an extravagant claim to make; do not all poets necessarily create their own language in order to express precisely particular thoughts and emotions? Sylvia Plath's aim, however, seems to be not just to find the right words to express herself. She wants to startle her readers into giving her their full attention; the lines of her verse are like a shout in a quiet room, making all heads turn in her direction. She achieves this by various means.

Her use of vivid imagery of the kind that makes the reader gasp in startled recognition is, of course, not unique to her. From the seventeenth-century Metaphysicals onwards poets have used startling juxtapositions, unexpected parallels, images that link the unexpected, just as Plath does:

> Then the flutings of their Ionian
> Death-gowns . . .

> ('Death & Co.')

> [the trees] Brood, rooted in their heaped losses.

> ('Parliament Hill Fields', *Crossing the Water*)

Sometimes there is a recklessness in her poems, especially in her later work, as if she were daring the reader to laugh at the deliberate clumsiness of expression, introduced to startle or to sound a jarring note:

> Barely daring to breathe or Achoo.

> ('Daddy')

> Attended by roses,

> By kisses, by cherubim,
> By whatever these pink things mean.

> ('Fever 103°')

In some poems, especially those in which she tries to exorcise her parents, she goes beyond the desire to startle. In such poems we find a deliberate intent to shock, notably in 'Berck-Plage', in the 'Daddy' poem, and above all in 'Medusa':

You steamed to me over the sea,
Fat and red, a placenta.

Who do you think you are?
A Communion wafer? Blubbery Mary?

Her use of colloquialisms, of slangy phrases has a different effect. In a grave, even tragic context such trite phrases change, acquire a new, shocking meaning. Thus Plath on suicide in 'Lady Lazarus':

I do it so it feels like hell.
I do it so it feels real.
I guess you could say I've a call.

Equally she can startle her readers by introducing quiet lines of the utmost simplicity and great beauty:

Love, love, my season.

('The Couriers')

Father, this thick air is murderous.
I would breathe water.

('Full Fathom Five', *The Colossus*)

Winter is for women.

('Wintering')

This is the light of the mind . . .

('The Moon and the Yew Tree')

In her complex, fraught poems the simplicity of such lines is quite startling. She demands, and receives, constant attention from her readers. Words ring out in her poems with such surprising effect that it almost seems as though they had never been used before. It appears likely that this is something that she consciously strove to achieve, highly aware as she was of the power and potency of the word. In one of her last poems, 'Words', written days before her death, she seems to be defining the poet's power in the opening lines:

Axes
After whose stroke the wood rings,
And the echoes!

There seems no better way of describing her achievement.

Part 5

Suggestions for further reading

Works by Sylvia Plath

Poetry:
Ariel, Faber, London, 1965; paperback 1968.
The Colossus and Other Poems, William Heinemann, London, 1960, reissued by Faber, London, 1967; paperback 1972.
Crossing the Water, Faber, London, 1971; paperback 1975.
Winter Trees, Faber, London, 1971; paperback 1975.
Collected Poems, Faber, London, 1981.
Selected Poems, chosen by Ted Hughes, Faber, London, 1985.

Prose:
The Bell Jar (by 'Victoria Lucas'), William Heinemann, London, 1963; (by Sylvia Plath) Faber Paperback, London, 1966.
Johnny Panic and the Bible of Dreams, Faber, London, 1977; paperback 1979. A collection of short stories, essays and journal entries.
The Bed Book, Faber, London, 1976; paperback 1986. A children's story.

Letters and journals:
Letters Home: Correspondence 1950–1963, selected and edited with commentary by Aurelia Schober-Plath, Faber, London, 1975; paperback 1978.
Journals, edited by Frances McCullough, consulting editor Ted Hughes, Dial Press, New York, 1982.

Biographies and critical studies

HAYMAN, RONALD: *The Death and Life of Sylvia Plath*, Heinemann, London, 1991. A biography with emphasis on Plath's obsession with death.

HOLBROOK, DAVID: *Sylvia Plath: Poetry and Existence*, The Athlone Press, London, 1976; paperback 1988. Over-emphasis on the psychological aspect of her work.
ROSE, JACQUELINE: *The Haunting of Sylvia Plath*, Virago, London, 1991. Plath's work (and her life) examined in the light of psychoanalysis.
STEVENSON, ANNE: *Bitter Fame: a Life of Sylvia Plath*, Viking, London, 1989.
WAGNER, LINDA W.: *Sylvia Plath, the Critical Heritage* (Critical Heritage Series), Routledge, London, 1988. A collection of essays and book reviews of Plath's work over the years by both British and American writers.
WAGNER-MARTIN, LINDA: *Sylvia Plath: a Biography*, Chatto & Windus, London, 1988.

Background reading

ADCOCK, FLEUR (ED.): *The Faber Book of 20th Century Women Poets*, Faber, London, 1987.
POSNER, CAROL; KEEFE, JOAN; WEAVER, KATHLEEN (EDS): *The Penguin Book of Women Poets*, Penguin Books, Harmondsworth, 1989.
VENDLER, HELEN (ED.): *The Faber Book of Contemporary American Poetry*, Faber, London, 1986.

The author of these notes

HANA SAMBROOK was educated at the Charles University in Prague and the University of Edinburgh. She worked as an editor in educational publishing and was for some years on the staff of the Edinburgh University Library. Now a freelance editor in London, she is the author of York Notes on *The Tenant of Wildfell Hall*, *Lark Rise to Candleford*, *Victory* and *My Family and Other Animals*.